PERSONALITIES *and* POWERS

LENIN

Liberator or Oppressor?

JOHN LAVER

Hodder & Stoughton

D0414189

Acknowledgements

The publishers would like to thank the following for their permission
to reproduce illustrations in this volume:

Novosti (London) cover; p. 38; p. 39; p. 52; p. 57; p. 71; p. 85.
Professor Stephen White p. 73; p. 93; p. 97.

Every effort has been made to trace and acknowledge ownership of
copyright. The publishers will be glad to make suitable
arrangements with any copyright holder whom it has not been
possible to contact.

British Library Cataloguing in Publication Data
Laver, John
  Lenin: liberator or oppressor?
  I. Title

ISBN 0-340-60281-3

First published 1994
Impression number   10   9   8   7   6   5   4   3   2   1
Year   1998   1997   1996   1995   1994

Typeset by Litho Link Ltd, Welshpool, Powys, Wales.
Printed in Great Britain for the Hodder and Stoughton Educational,
a division of Hodder Headline Plc, Mill Road, Dunton Green, Sevenoaks,
Kent TN13 2YA by St Edmundsbury Press, Bury St Edmunds.

CONTENTS

PREFACE

This book considers Lenin and his influence during his lifetime and later. Attention is devoted to both his actions and his ideas, since both were equally important, although not always at the same time. When I first studied the Russian Revolution as a student, I saw Lenin very much as the man of action, with clearly-defined views, and essentially the personification of the Bolshevik Party. I came to realise that this was a simplistic interpretation, and both Lenin's character and the issues connected with his impact upon Russian, Soviet and world history were far more complex than appeared at first sight.

Prominence is given to Lenin's formative years, about which he himself was very reticent; the struggles within his own movement, frequently glossed over by Soviet historians; and his years in power and decline. His historical reputation will also be assessed.

This study does not pretend to be, and indeed cannot be, a history of Russia during Lenin's lifetime. It assumes that students have at least a basic knowledge of Russian and Soviet history during the years of Lenin's life, and there are many accessible books on the subject. This particular book is concerned very much with Lenin the man, the thinker, and the politician. I have focused on those areas of Lenin's life and career which seem to be of most significance. Although I have considered the interpretations of some eminent journalists and historians, the conclusions I draw are my own. They may therefore provoke disagreement, and indeed it would be strange if all interpretations of Lenin were the same. Some of my own interpretations have changed over the years: facts are facts, but judgements change in the light of experience and new evidence.

The changes in the former Soviet Union make the study of Lenin no less significant than in the days of the monolithic Communist State. I hope that the views expressed in this study will provoke further thought and discussion, as reading other historians on Lenin has stimulated my own interest.

Thanks are due to Julie Laver for advice and support during the writing of this book.

INTRODUCTION

Vladimir Lenin was in power in the Soviet Union for less than seven years, between the October Revolution of 1917 and his early death in January 1924. Yet as leader of the world's first Marxist State, he will always occupy a prominent position in the history of the twentieth century, both outside as well as within the borders of his own country. The Soviet Union bore Lenin's imprint, although he would not have approved of or even have recognised some of the changes which took place in succeeding generations. Such was Lenin's reputation at the time of his death, his name was often attached to later developments in order to give them a legitimacy in the eyes of their instigators. Lenin's influence also reached way beyond Russia. Communists in other countries acknowledged Lenin as a mentor and inspiration. Even today, with a re-evaluation of his career in the aftermath of the break-up of the old Soviet Union, Lenin remains a subject of great historical interest, as is often the fate of those who are important as symbols as well as human beings.

Lenin's story is a remarkable one. Although he came from a privileged background by contemporary Russian standards, his early enthusiasm for revolutionary change made him an outsider. He was obliged to spend many years in foreign exile. There was little to suggest in his early years that his optimistic vision of a Socialist utopia would be realised in his lifetime. Towards the end of his life he gave indications that he himself had doubts about its feasibility. And yet it would be wrong to describe him as a failure. He was an adept conspirator and manipulator of people and ideas, but only within a relatively small circle. He had no practical experience of administration or politics on the grand scale. Despite this, he arrived back in Russia in 1917 from relative obscurity to seize control of a large Empire, and then defend his precarious position in the face of a hostile world, with a small group of committed supporters. With supreme confidence he took over the reins of administration. He adapted his ideas and policies, and became concerned about trends of which he disapproved in the new Russia. He bequeathed an uncertain future to his successors: Lenin's Russia had already undergone considerable changes in six years and there was a commitment to further radical change.

Lenin was as important in the world of political ideas as of practical politics. Those ideas lived on, to be continually reinterpreted by Socialists and Communists throughout the world. Lenin's additions to Marxism created a body of ideas called Marxism-Leninism, which became the creed of many future revolutionary movements.

Lenin's name and reputation were enshrined by succeeding Soviet regimes so that he became in death an icon and banner to inspire future generations and justify Government or Party dictates. So Lenin was as important in death as in life. Yet the image, the propaganda, the distortions, all have rendered difficult the task of understanding this many-faceted man who died only a few years after what seemed, in 1917, to have been his greatest triumph.

ONE STEP FORWARDS, TWO STEPS BACK

CHILDHOOD AND SCHOOLING

Vladimir Ilyich Ulyanov was born on 22 April 1870 in the Russian provincial town of Simbirsk, on the great river Volga. He was born into the intelligentsia, a privileged class in nineteenth-century Russia, and one which believed implicitly in the value of education. Ulyanov's father, Ilya, had the year before changed his profession from that of physics teacher to that of Inspector for Elementary Schools for Simbirsk province. His promotion advanced the family to the status of gentry, and the children were always to speak in the style of the Russian nobility. Before his death in 1886 Ilya was to become Director of Elementary Schools for the region. Ilya was respectable, conservative and devout. In 1863 he had married Maria Alexandrovna, daughter of a physician. Maria was self-educated but talented, and her talents were to be reflected in Vladimir Ulyanov. There was non-Russian blood in Ulyanov's grandparents, but this does not seem to have noticably affected his outlook in later life.

We are not certain of all the details of Ulyanov's early years. For one thing, in later life he showed little interest in revealing autobiographical details. For another, during the years of Stalin's dictatorship, evidence was doctored in the interests of the regime. However, some facts are well established. The young Ulyanov was one of six children. Anna was born in 1864, Alexander in 1866, Vladimir himself four years later, Olga in 1871, Dimitri in 1874, and Maria in 1878. The family was well-off by contemporary Russian standards. Vladimir was a lively child, taught by his mother until he entered school at the age of nine. He appears to have been far more unruly than his brothers and sisters. A short and sturdy boy, he frequently caused mayhem in the family household. As he grew, he tried to emulate his older brother Alexander, perhaps jealous of the latter's status as the family favourite.

At school, in contrast to his antics at home, Vladimir proved to be a conscientious and meticulous pupil. This element of dual personality persisted with him throughout his life: a delight in hard work and intellectual arguments was balanced by a love of outdoor activities, the more strenuous the better. His peers commented upon the systematic presentation of his work and his powers of concentration. As a student he was particularly gifted in languages, history, geography and literature. The headmaster at Simbirsk High School remarked upon his 'unusual carefulness and industry' and his 'systematic thought'. Ironically, the headmaster was the father of the Alexander Kerensky who was to be one of Lenin's great protagonists in 1917.

When not studying Ulyanov enjoyed the country sports of skating, skiing, fishing and swimming. He also recited poetry and sang songs with his family at home, or went on long rambles. It was a near idyllic childhood, with no indication of the turbulence to come. Although the death of Ulyanov's father in 1886 was a blow to the teenage son, the resulting legacy enabled the family to live relatively comfortably, even to the extent of allowing Ulyanov the luxury of several trips abroad.

THE RUSSIA OF LENIN'S YOUTH

What was the Russia of Ulyanov's youth like? The family lived out a comfortable existence during the 1870s and early 1880s, in a country whose social and political structure seemed stable. Tsar Alexander II was, in true Russian tradition, 'an autocratic and unlimited monarch', ordained to rule by God alone. Ministers and bureaucrats were responsible only to the Tsar. His power was augmented by the fact that he was also titular head of the Orthodox Church. Alexander II had initiated several reforms in the early 1860s. These had included the abolition of serfdom, and a series of legal, social, administrative and military measures which had appeared to give Russia the trappings of a modern state. But, by contemporary Western European standards, Russia remained a reactionary and backward colossus.

Over three-quarters of the Russian population were peasants. Whilst they no longer had the status of serfs after 1861, the peasants were burdened with long-term debts owed in return for the land which they had been granted after emancipation; and their lives were ruled by the village commune or 'mir'. A rapid increase in the rural population created additional pressures, and poverty and uncertainty were widespread. Farming techniques were generally antiquated, and productivity was low.

Russian industry too was backward. The Russian Government was not yet in a position to exploit the country's huge natural resources. Although there were increases in output in some sectors, including coal and steel, and the rate of industrial expansion was to be quickened by Government intervention in the 1890s, the overall economic climate was one of stagnation.

Russia's social structure reflected the economic pattern. The mass of the peasantry was uneducated; there was a small working class or proletariat in the few centres of industry; there was a small educated middle class; and a numerically tiny aristocratic élite, which for the most part possessed great wealth. Some of the educated élite was dissatisfied with the autocratic system of government, and looked to Europe rather than its homeland for its cultural nourishment. Educated intellectuals debated whether Europe should be admired for its civil and political liberties, or despised as an alien force and a possible threat to the traditions of a rural and communal Russia.

The 1870s in Russia witnessed the growth of a revolutionary movement which believed in peasant Socialism, based upon a communal way of life, and one which would enable Russia to escape the large-scale capitalist development which had been a characteristic of western European economies, and had led to the development of great cities and new social problems. Intellectuals who espoused these ideas were known as populists or narodniks. Their attempts to persuade peasants to their way of thinking were largely unproductive.

Alexander II's reforms had been introduced in the wake of Russia's defeat in the Crimean War. They had been a response to perceived weaknesses in administrative, military and financial structures, and an awareness of developing social tensions. With hindsight, we might conclude that the reforms were inadequate: the aristocracy resented the lessening of its powers over the peasantry; and the peasants themselves gained little other than their nominal freedom. The Government relinquished little of its real power, and so the discontent of alienated groups simply grew, and branched into new forms such as Marxism. When it came to the crunch, Alexander II, and his successor Alexander III, opted for repression in response to criticism. And yet Tsarism as an institution was to survive for many more years. The Ulyanov family, living a life which was privileged by the standards of most Russians, could not have anticipated the great traumas soon to descend upon it.

A MARTYR TO THE CAUSE

The comfortable existence of the Ulyanov family came to an abrupt end in 1887. In that year Alexander was arrested and tried for high treason. In addition to studying zoology at university, the student Alexander had been manufacturing bombs and plotting revolution. He had become the leader of a group of St Petersburg terrorists, attracted by the tactics of the group 'People's Will'. It was in Alexander's apartment that the assassination of Tsar Alexander III had been planned for 1 March 1887. The planned date was actually brought forward, but the plot was foiled by a vigilant secret police. Instead of emulating the assassination of Alexander II, which had occurred in 1881, Alexander and his friends were arrested. Fifteen men were tried for the attempted assassination. Alexander's mother Maria travelled to the capital and after several weeks was able to meet her son, who defiantly stood by his revolutionary principles.

At his trial Alexander tried to shoulder all responsibility for the plot, and repeated his belief that terror was a legitimate political instrument in a repressive state, and that 'there is no death more honourable than death for the common good'. He was found guilty of high treason, refused to plead for clemency, and together with four comrades was hanged in Schlusselburg fortress in May 1887.

THE MAKING OF A REVOLUTIONARY

The news of Alexander's execution reached Vladimir Ulyanov soon afterwards. He is supposed to have declared: 'I'll make them pay for this! I swear it!' With an iron determination astonishing in one so young, he sat his school exams during the week following the execution, and won a gold medal.

It is sometimes claimed that the execution of his brother was the cataclysmic event that put the impressionable younger brother on the road to revolution. However, traumatic as the experience undoubtedly was, the more so since the Ulyanov family heard of Alexander's sentence only after it had been carried out, Vladimir had already shown signs of reacting against his orthodox and respectable upbringing. He claimed in later life that he had suddenly abandoned his belief in God at the age of sixteen. In his younger days he had attended church with his father. Whether the conversion to atheism was a reaction against an orthodox background, or whether it was the conclusion to an internal intellectual struggle, it is impossible to know. What we can say is that Ulyanov began to display a mixture of confidence and certainty typical of his career. He was able to change his intellectual stance with no apparent residue of doubt.

It was at this time that Vladimir certainly showed an interest in studying the ideas which had turned his brother into a martyr. Like Alexander, he developed a lifelong devotion to the literary work of Chernyshevsky. One of the generation of intellectuals disillusioned by the failure of the 1848 revolutions, Chernyshevsky wrote a book called *What is to be Done?*, which influenced many educated persons of Lenin's generation. He compiled detailed data in his criticism of Russian society, and distrusted the notion of reform from above. According to Cherny- shevsky, History was about class struggle, and the state was bound to be the instrument of the dominant class. Unlike Marx, he did not see capitalism as an essential stage in the historical process, and retained a utopian belief in the peasant and small producer, whilst at the same time believing in a form of state Socialism. Chernyshevsky was full of contradictions, but his writings influenced the young Ulyanov, who was also attracted by the idea of emulating the austere, slightly romantic revolutionary stereotype. Ulyanov also began to read the political writings of the Russian narodniks or populists, and despite his later criticism of such writings, he was certainly influenced by their ideas, and they merged with his Marxism.

STUDENT RADICAL

—

Although Ulyanov was already a marked man, being the brother of a convicted terrorist, he was admitted to his local university at Kazan in the autumn of 1887. Probably his exemplary school record stood him in good stead. If that was the case, his superiors were in for a shock, for the new student was anxious to prove that he was no longer a model student. The would-be lawyer lasted only four months before being sent down with several fellow students for taking part in demonstrations. In December 1887 the student body had presented a list of demands to the dean. Ulyanov was prominent in the delegation. He was unrepentant as he was expelled from the university and the city, declaring that 'My road has been laid out by my elder brother'. The university authorities commented upon his attitude:

> He attracted attention by his secretiveness, inattentiveness and indeed rudeness . . . In view of the exceptional circumstances of the Ulyanov family, such behaviour by Ulyanov . . . gave reason to believe him fully capable of unlawful and criminal demonstrations of all kinds.

There was nothing unusual in student unrest in Russia. As budding intellectuals, it was natural for young students to react against a regime which reinforced authoritarianism with censorship and political repression. The students were influenced by Russian populist sentiments, not Marxism. The regime actually acted relatively leniently in the case of Ulyanov, although they did ban him from going abroad to study. His mother persuaded the authorities to allow her son to live on her estate at Kokushkino. Here Ulyanov could read widely and indulge his liking for outdoor sports. Although under police supervision, within a year he was allowed back in Kazan, but not to the university. The Ulyanov family rented a small house in Kazan, and it was here that Ulyanov first read Marx and was converted to his principles. Thereafter he steadfastly maintained that Marx's arguments were scientific and irrefutable. Soon he was trying to convert his friends also. Ulyanov now abandoned the narodnik idea that capitalism was an unwelcome development. Rather, like Marx, he saw it as preparing the path for Socialism. Where he was to diverge from Marx was in his growing belief that the workers themselves were unlikely to develop a Socialist philosophy without leadership from the intelligentsia, and, perhaps because of Russian conditions, Ulyanov was more prepared to countenance violence as a political weapon, although he doubted the value of individual acts of terrorism such as had attracted his brother.

THE YOUNG LAWYER

Ulyanov's mother did not approve of his political activities, but nevertheless made every effort to get her son readmitted to the university. When the Kazan authorities refused, she approached the Ministry of Education in St Petersburg. Her persistence was rewarded when Ulyanov was permitted to register as an external student at St Petersburg University and to take his law examinations there.

Ulyanov's stay in the capital was short, but he passed his examinations in 1891. He was awarded first-class honours and was top of the list of 33 external students. Of more significance, he made contact with a group of Marxists. Having also read his dead brother's copy of *Das Kapital*, which an uncomprehending censor had allowed into Russia, and having studied political economy for his examinations, Ulyanov was well educated in subversive opinions.

Ulyanov was now qualified to practise law. His success thus far was marred by the death from typhoid fever of his sister Olga, who was also studying in St Petersburg. Ulyanov got permission to move to Samara, in the middle Volga region, and he set up as assistant to a barrister in January 1892. His boss doubled as his chess partner. During 1892 Ulyanov handled at least 12 cases of petty crime, but he seemed more interested in the underground Marxist club which he started in Samara. Amongst his early converts here were his remaining siblings, Dimitri, Anna and Maria.

In 1892 Samara experienced famine. Ulyanov encountered peasants who came to the city in search of food. But he did not join the bourgeois citizens who organised charity for the starving. Ulyanov's stance was uncompromising and based not upon a short-term emotional response to a human tragedy, but a careful analysis of the political, economic and social order which, in his opinion, allowed such tragedies to occur:

The famine threatens to create serious disturbances and possibly the destruction of the entire bourgeois order. Hence the efforts of the well-to-do to mitigate the effect of the famine are quite natural . . . *Psychologically this talk of feeding the starving is nothing but an expression of the saccharine sweet sentimentality so characteristic of our intelligentsia.*

This was to be a typical Lenin paradox: a man capable of considerable warmth in personal relations, but on a wider political stage a man concerned only with arguing a case forcibly, and concerned above all with systems and concepts rather than the fate of individuals. Ulyanov dated the beginning of his revolutionary career from this period in Samara.

SUBVERSION IN ST PETERSBURG

In 1893 the Ulyanov family moved again, this time to Moscow. But Ulyanov himself returned to St Petersburg. Although on the surface practising law, he was more heavily engaged than ever in political activity. At first he concentrated on reading. But he was to join an underground Marxist organisation called the 'Elders'. It was probably at this time that he first came into contact with real proletarians. St Petersburg was the fastest growing industrial city in Europe. Thousands of workers, many of them ex-peasants, flocked to the large factories to work in appalling conditions. Some joined study circles in which Ulyanov and his colleagues expounded their political beliefs.

Throughout his life Ulyanov was engaged in arguments about both theory and tactics. This was already evident in the early days. Many of the early Russian Marxists, reacting against what they saw as the unscientific, emotionally-inspired activities of the Populists, urged the workers whom they taught to keep out of illegal strikes, which could not serve a long-term political purpose. Ulyanov though was dissatisfied, and wanted more action. He wrote leaflets for striking workers. Not that Ulyanov wished to act alone: his first large-scale work, written in 1894 and entitled *What Are the Friends of the People?*, argued for the foundation of a Russian Social-Democrat party.

Ulyanov converted some of his colleagues and became leader of the

Elders. A colleague from these early days, Alexander Potresov, penned a succinct portrait of 'the old man', as the 25-year-old Ulyanov was already known:

> His face was worn; his entire head bald, except for some thin hair at the temples, and he had a scanty reddish beard. His squinting eyes peered slyly from under his brows . . . his voice sounded old and hoarse.

Life held its pleasures for the young revolutionary. He did very little legal work, living primarily off a monthly allowance from his mother. He spent the summer of 1894 in the countryside, with relatives. Back in the city, he met his future wife.

In 1895 Ulyanov travelled abroad to meet both foreign Socialists and Plekhanov, the most prominent of the early Russian Marxists. Ulyanov discussed many issues with Plekhanov at Geneva, but although he admired the older man, Plekhanov was soon to be pushed into the background, his philosophical temperament unable to keep pace with the dynamism of Ulyanov, the man of action. And yet Plekhanov sensed the qualities of Ulyanov the politician.

Soon afterwards Ulyanov travelled to Zurich to meet Axelrod, another revered figure from the early days of Russian Social Democracy. A week of discussions led Axelrod to conclude, like Plekhanov, that Ulyanov possessed an unusual combination of theoretical ability and practical organisational skills, and should therefore be encouraged in his political ambitions.

ARREST AND SIBERIAN EXILE

Ulyanov returned to St Petersburg in September 1895. Under close scrutiny by the secret police, a 'League for the Struggle for the Emancipation of the Working Class' was set up. Ulyanov prepared the first edition of an underground newspaper, whilst writing begging letters to his mother for money to eke out his frugal existence in the capital – he now had very few legal clients. In December, before the newspaper was printed, Ulyanov and several of his associates were arrested.

Ulyanov's first imprisonment in St Petersburg was not an unduly harsh experience. He was regularly visited by his sisters and he had access to books. He was able to communicate with fellow members of the League outside prison, writing to them in invisible ink. He played chess with fellow-inmates of the prison by means of a wall-tapping code. Through a regime of physical exercise he kept himself fit. He also started a major work, *The Development of Capitalism in Russia* and practised the foreign languages in which he was to become very proficient.

After 14 months in prison, Ulyanov began a three-year exile in the Siberian village of Shushenskoe, in May 1897. It was a relatively easy existence, with an allowance from the Government and the opportunity to read, write and exercise to his heart's content. He became a popular figure in the village. He refused his mother's request to come and live near him, but continued to take her money. He studied and exercised with an equal intensity.

Whilst at Shushenskoe Ulyanov wrote to a schoolteacher, Nadezhda Krupskaya, asking her to join him and marry him. The two had met four years before in St Petersburg and had communicated during his prison term. She was a strong-willed individual, but shared enough of Ulyanov's beliefs for her to be an acceptable companion. Having married in exile, one of their first joint projects was to translate into Russian a trade union history by the English Socialist couple, Beatrice and Sydney Webb.

Krupskaya was an intelligent woman and already a revolutionary in her own right, but she was the ideal wife for Ulyanov, acting as his secretary and subordinating her own career to his, although she was to have an important role as an official in the People's Commissariat of Education in post-revolutionary Russia.

Ulyanov became the focal point for other political exiles in the region and the busy life of political debate, reading, writing and exercise continued unabated. It was during this period that Ulyanov both reinforced his theoretical grounding in the politics and economics of his country, and projected plans for future political action. These plans included the development of a Social Democratic Party, and were to be refined in his later work *What is to be Done?* He also became involved at a distance in controversy about Marxist philosophy, which was interpreted in different ways by revolutionaries. The first use of the name 'Lenin' occurred in this period – appearing on the title page of the book *The Aims of Russian Social Democrats*, which was published in Switzerland. The alias, assumed by Ulyanov in order to confuse the police, was probably taken from the name of the River Lena in Siberia, and henceforth will be used in this book for Ulyanov.

While in exile Lenin heard the news that a Congress of revolutionaries meeting in Minsk in March 1898 had agreed on the formation of the Russian Social-Democratic Labour Party, complete with a Central Committee. Soon afterwards Lenin wrote his *Project for Our Party's Programme*, in which he outlined his beliefs on the development of capitalism in Russia, and listed his proposed social reforms.

FOREIGN EXILE

In March 1900 Lenin was allowed to return to European Russia, but not to St Petersburg. He soon left for Switzerland in order to supervise the publication of a Social Democratic newspaper, to be smuggled into Russia. Lenin was on the editorial board of *Iskra* (The Spark) – the first edition of which appeared in December 1900. The period of long foreign exile had begun. It was to be a period punctuated by times of optimism and false dawns, but throughout it Lenin never ceased to live the life of a dedicated professional revolutionary, confident that one day his version of Marxism would prevail.

One reason why Lenin was keen to be involved in *Iskra* was the existence of different interpretations of Marxism among the Marxist emigrés scattered throughout Europe. Through *Iskra* Lenin was able to impose his own views on the new movement, or at least attempt to. Lenin was more concerned that the various Marxist groups, rather than proletarians, read *Iskra*. The importance which Lenin attached to the newspaper can be gauged by the fact that he wrote three articles for the first edition, and he produced 29 copies of *Iskra* during the next two years. Copies of *Iskra* and revolutionary pamphlets were smuggled into Russia and distributed by enthusiastic but often naive young revolutionaries, in factories, streets and other public places. It was dangerous work, but the message was gradually spread as workers themselves became involved in the movement and in turn worked on their comrades.

Krupskaya was allowed out of Russia and rejoined Lenin in Munich. The collaboration was resumed, although production problems with *Iskra* caused the couple to move to London in April 1902. A flat was rented in Kings Cross. The *Iskra* editorial board was re-assembled. Lenin took the opportunity to improve his English by involving himself in the life of the locality. London made a great impression on him. Krupskaya described their wanderings:

> He liked the bustle of this huge commercial city . . . the quiet squares, the detached houses, with their separate entrances and shining windows adorned with greenery, the drives frequented only by highly polished broughams, were much in evidence, but tucked away nearby, the mean little streets, inhabited by the London working people, where lines with washing hung across the street, and pale children played in the gutter – these sites could not be seen from the bus top. In such districts we went on foot, and observing these glaring con-trasts of wealth and poverty, Ilyich would mutter between clenched teeth, in English, 'Two nations!'

London was also notable for Lenin's first meeting with Leon Trotsky. Trotsky obviously impressed the older man, because Lenin pressed him to stay and work on *Iskra*, although Plekhanov and other senior Social Democrats were less enthusiastic about Trotsky's credentials.

WHAT IS TO BE DONE?

All the while Lenin was honing his ideas on the possibility of a Socialist revolution. *What is to be Done?* was begun in mid 1901 and completed in February 1902. Its publication was to mark a significant stage in the development of the Russian revolutionary movement and Lenin's career, although he had already been formulating his ideas on Party organisation during the period of Siberian exile.

'Revolutionary movement' is something of a misnomer, since there had been several different revolutionary strands in nineteenth-century Russia, frequently in opposition to each other. During the 1850s and 1860s many Russian revolutionaries looked to the peasants for Russia's salvation. The noble peasant, whose communal mode of existence supposedly enshrined the human virtues, was idealised. Capitalism was condemned as having introduced an alien and destructive social force into this idyll. Some of these Russian populists, disillusioned with their lack of progress, became anarchists, opposing ordered government as well as capitalism. For many, anti-capitalism was also bound up with a nationalism which exalted Russia's uniqueness and opposed Western influences.

Attempts to convert the peasants to a Socialist way of thinking and later acts of terrorism, such as the assassination of Alexander II in 1881, did not appear to have seriously weakened the regime. But a new force was at work. An industrial revolution took off in Russia in the 1890s, and many peasants flocked to the factories or bought the products of capitalism rather than rejecting them. This led a number of populists, Plekhanov among them, to focus their attention on the new proletariat. Marxism seemed to offer a relevant tool to analyse this phenomenon, particularly since it combined a supposed scientific analysis of social and economic systems with a messianic belief in a better future. Plekhanov and his ilk did not believe that a Socialist revolution was imminent: Russia had first to experience a bourgeois revolution which would establish a parliamentary democracy, which in turn would create new opportunities for the working class and in turn pave the way for Socialism. It was far easier for Russian Marxists to go on to forge links with their Socialist counterparts in the more advanced western European countries since, unlike the old populists, they shared the same basic beliefs.

Where did Lenin fit into this pattern? Plekhanov had attempted to create Marxist organisations in Russia, but he was operating from abroad, and was a better theorist than he was man of action. Lenin combined practical and theoretical skills. This was just as well, since he became embroiled in controversies about the tactics and direction of the revolutionary movement. Some of the arguments were important only to the protagonists themselves; others had a longer-term significance.

One faction which Lenin encountered was 'Economism'. This label was attached to the view that the revolutionary movement should concentrate on practical measures to help the proletariat, such as fighting for higher wages. The political struggle against tsarism could be left for the time being to the middle class. The chief proponents of this view in the 1890s were S Prokopovich and his wife E Kuskova. Lenin strongly condemned such views, since they implied that revolutionaries should forget about politics and seek to improve material life through the formation of trade unions, co-operative societies and other working-class organisations as in western Europe. To Lenin this smacked of compromise with the regime and its economic and social structure.

Lenin was similarly appalled by a development in the German Social Democrat Party, the largest of its type in Europe. Led by Edward Bernstein, a number of German Socialists opposed the idea of violent revolution and advocated a gradual and peaceful transition to Socialism.

Lenin attacked such heretical views through the columns of *Iskra* and other writings with passionate intensity. His concern for ideological purity, paradoxical given that Marx himself had left neither a consistent canon of thought nor a blueprint for revolution, became inextricably linked with his views on Party organisation, one of the original features of Leninism. A tightly-knit Party organisation would facilitate guardian-ship of the torch of ideological purity. Lenin's views were elaborated in *What is to be Done?*.

Lenin displayed a wider European awareness not common among his colleagues. He considered the German situation, then concluded that the Russian one was different. Without parliamentary democracy, a mass party in Russia was an impossibility. Nor was it desirable: the German Social Democratic Party was large and well represented in Parliament, but its rapid expansion in membership had, in Lenin' eyes, caused it to dilute its Marxist purity. In Lenin's opinion, such mass parties were liable to seek compromises with the system rather than overthrow it, a view which the German Socialists confirmed by supporting the raising of war credits by their Government in 1914.

Lenin argued instead for a Party of professional revolutionaries. Characteristically, he called upon authorities such as Engels, already dead, to support his arguments. The Social Democratic Party was to be leader of the movement for change. Its task was to spread agitation amongst all social classes. When the tsarist regime was overthrown, a fully-fledged capitalist system could develop in Russia, the necessary precondition for Socialism. Lenin claimed that the Russian working class lacked the political awareness to achieve this for itself. Therefore, middle-class intellectuals like himself – and Marx and Engels before him – were needed to provide leadership and political education.

The most original and important section of *What is to be Done?* concerned Lenin's views on Party organisation. A disciplined Party was essential in a repressive society in which police agents infiltrated dissident groups. It would also inhibit the spread of heresies like Economism. Marx had not written much about revolutionary parties, but Lenin argued for full-time professional activists, subject to internal controls and direction from the centre, as the only guarantee of survival in a hostile climate. Lenin did not decry the efforts of mass trade unions to better the material conditions of their members, he simply insisted that political action as such should be the separate preserve of the Party. Lenin also emphasised the importance of a central Party organ, the function of *Iskra*.

Lenin was not the most fluent of writers, and he railed ungenerously at political opponents with whom he disagreed. Yet he did come up with some striking phrases, such as 'Give us an organisation of revolutionaries, and we will turn Russia upside down!' It should be remembered that Lenin was not creating literature but was writing a manual for fellow activists. The book was circulated unobtrusively after its publication in March 1902. It is difficult to assess how many people read it first-hand, but certainly most revolutionaries in Russia and emigrés abroad were soon aware of its arguments. These attracted a strong response both positive and negative. Later, hostile, commentators have discovered the germs of Stalinist excesses in this book. Certainly the concept of a revolution made by an élite on behalf of a suppressed and submerged working class might be viewed as harbouring the germ of dictatorship. It is also true that Lenin leaves certain awkward questions unanswered: if, for example, the élite is to be secret and conspiratorial, what restraints exist to prevent the leader or leaders exercising power arbitrarily? However, the arguments were being put forward in a police state, and little thought was given to the post-revolutionary scenario, only to the means of bringing about revolution. It may be fair to accuse Lenin of naivety in ignoring these issues or perhaps assuming that they would simply resolve themselves, but probably wide of the mark to accuse him of directly paving the way to Stalinist authoritarianism *at this stage*.

What concerned many of Lenin's critics at the time was what they viewed as his tendency to underestimate the potential contribution of the proletariat. For example, Axelrod claimed that Lenin saw the working class as pawns, to be used by intellectual Marxists pursuing their own ends. Rosa Luxemburg, a leading German Communist, was suspicious of 'bureaucratic centralism', a condition under which rank and file Party members were unable to monitor and criticise the behaviour of their leaders. Ironically, this was an issue which was to concern Lenin himself towards the end of his life. Trotsky also feared that Lenin might repeat the mistake of the Russian populists in isolating Party leaders from their ordinary supporters.

Lenin did answer his critics. In *Letter to a Comrade About Our Organisational Tasks* he insisted that he did want workers to join the Party. But he argued that there were different levels of membeship and commitment. The hard core would be full-time professionals, who inevitably would exert most authority. Part-time activists and ordinary Party members would have their place, but could not expect to know all that was going on or to exercise the same powers. Although Lenin insisted that the Central Committee of the Party should not have unrestrained powers, he did not explain satisfactorily how this could be avoided in the structure which he envisaged.

Lenin's capacity to provoke controversy spilled over into disagreements with the other *Iskra* editors, who were formulating their own Party rules. Some colleagues, such as Martov, were already of the opinion that Lenin was ambitious for personal control of the revolutionary movement. When Plekhanov submitted his ideas for a Party programme in 1902, Lenin argued over some points, although the two men agreed on the fundamentals of Socialist development, that is, they foresaw a period of 'bourgeois rule' followed by a 'Dictatorship of the Proletariat'. Lenin was difficult to work with. Potresov, who actually allied himself with Lenin in some of the disputes, declared of him:

> he was incapable of co-operating with other people. It went against his grain.

THE BOLSHEVIK MOVEMENT IS BORN: THE 1903 CONGRESS

In April 1903 Lenin moved to Geneva, but a return to London was not long in coming. The increasing number of arguments about policy and tactics in the Social Democratic movement led the *Iskra* board to summon a Second Congress. This Congress met in Brussels in July 1903, but difficulties and the threat of police intervention caused the delegates to transfer proceedings to London. There were 43 delegates, very few of them workers, representing different points of view. Lenin immediately launched into the attack by proposing structural changes to the Party leadership which would have put the *Iskra* group in control. Lenin lost one motion to Martov, concerning rules of Party membership, but Lenin carried the majority on other important issues, assisted by the authority of Plekhanov's support. A single Party organisation was to replace the various independent organisations. The *Iskra* group was in control, as other delegates walked out. Thus Lenin's majority, the 'Bolsheviks', defeated Martov's minority, the 'Mensheviks'. Lenin consolidated his victory by having the *Iskra* board reduced in numbers to eliminate Martov's supporters. It was the sort of political in-fighting at which the dogged Lenin excelled.

FURTHER PARTY IN-FIGHTING

The 1903 Congress was significant in several respects. Lenin had set out his tactics and principles clearly. The Mensheviks, arguing in favour of a more loosely-organised parliamentary-style Party, encouraging the recruitment of as many factory workers as possible, had been defeated. Theirs was a philosophy more suited to the democratic parliamentary tradition of western Europe. The Bolsheviks certainly drew upon an earlier revolutionary tradition for inspiration, but were gearing their tactics to the realities of the situation in Russia. Can the origins of the post-revolutionary one-Party state be traced back to the 1903 split? To think Lenin's victory in 1917 with his victory in 1903 would be simplistic. Lenin had established a basis for his revolutionary programme, but victory was a long way off. Difficulties arose for Lenin immediately after the Congress: Plekhanov came to regard Lenin as too belligerent and divisive. He was also upset by reports of Lenin's disrespectful comments about himself, Plekhanov. Other colleagues wanted a reconciliation between the factions. Lenin refused to compromise, and resigned from the editorship of *Iskra*. However, he arranged for his supporters to co-opt him on to the Party's Central Committee. Lenin was causing great annoyance to many colleagues, who regarded him as the biggest obstacle to re-unifying the movement. In 1905 the Bolsheviks and Mensheviks were to hold separate Congresses. Some Social Democrats, both within and beyond Russia, took issue with Lenin's philosophy. Trotsky went as far as to parody Lenin's views on the Party:

> The Party's organisation takes the place of the Party itself; the Central Committee takes the place of the Party's organisation; and finally 'the dictator' takes the place of the Central Committee.

a note on . . .

PRINCIPAL OPPOSITION GROUPS IN EARLY TWENTIETH-CENTURY RUSSIA

SOCIALIST REVOLUTIONARIES

These descended from the Populist movements of the 1870s. They won considerable support from the peasantry, although they also gained many working-class adherents in the 1900s. Their principal aim was to introduce a form of peasant Socialism, based upon the traditional village commune. Their tactics veered between individual acts of terrorism such as political assassinations, and political participation in the Dumas after the 1905 Revolution. The SRs became an organised political grouping in 1900, and adopted a programme in 1906. The growth in popular support for the SRs culminated in their impressive showing in the elections to the Constituent Assembly after the October Revolution. However, by then they had already split into Left and Right factions, and were soon to be suppressed by the Communists. The SR leader was Chernov, who joined the Provisional Government in 1917, emigrated in 1920, and eventually died in the United States in 1952.

SOCIAL DEMOCRATS

The RSDLP (All-Russian Social Democratic Labour Party) was founded at Minsk in 1898. In 1903, at the Party's Congress in London, a faction led by Lenin won a majority (hence the term *Bolsheviks*) in debates with a faction led by Martov (the minority or *Mensheviks*). The Mensheviks favoured a broadly-based popular revolutionary movement. Lenin argued instead for a disciplined, élite Party of professional revolutionaries. The split between the two factions steadily widened and became irreversible by 1917. Martov left Russia in 1921 and died in exile in Berlin in 1923.

The SDs were Marxists, and looked to the industrial working class or proletariat to be the prime movers in a Socialist revolution, although Lenin also tried to appeal to the peasantry. As Marxists, the SDs believed in certain laws of economic and social development. A bourgeois, democratic state would be established in the first stage of revolution. Only later would a Socialist Republic emerge.

The Bolsheviks made increased inroads into Menshevik support in the years prior to the 1917 Revolution. Leading Bolsheviks in 1917 included Lenin, Kamenev and Zinoviev. Trotsky only threw in his lot with the Bolsheviks after May 1917. Prominent Mensheviks included Martov and Sukhanov, who wrote a detailed first-hand account of the dramatic events of 1917.

LIBERALS

Liberals were not organised politically until the early 1900s, when two principal groups emerged: the moderate Octobrists, and the more radical Constitutional Democrats (Kadets). These groups comprised intellectuals and members of the gentry, professionals and industrialists. They wanted a Western-style parliament which would introduce liberal capitalist economic policies. Liberals faced the difficult situation of trying to force an obstinate Tsar to make important changes, without at the same time opening the floodgates to a revolution which would destroy the foundations of society. Both Liberal groups were represented in the Provisional Government. Prince Lvov and Milyukov were prominent Liberals, but their failure to preserve the regime established after the February Revolution was just the start of the rapid decline of their prospects and influence, and Liberal groups were soon to be silenced after the October Revolution.

Lenin answered his critics with characteristic self-confidence. In *One Step Forward, Two Steps Back*, published in 1904, he repeated the message of *What is to be Done?* but claimed that workers were welcome into the vanguard of the Party. This clarification of his position won Lenin some support in Social Democrat circles. Yet he was still a relatively isolated figure among the leading Social Democrat spirits. Despite the tenacity which Lenin displayed throughout his career, for a time now he was close to a state of nervous collapse. He recuperated with Krupskaya in Switzerland, walking in the mountains.

Refreshed, in December 1904 Lenin launched a new paper to challenge *Iskra*, as the voice of the proletariat. The paper was called *Vpered* (Forward). Lenin's spirits were further uplifted by the outbreak of the Russo-Japanese War, a prelude to the 1905 Revolution. The opportunity for immediate political action was high on the agenda, and made the theoretical arguments about Marxism seem less important. Nevertheless, they still provoked debate, and Lenin produced theoretical arguments to justify his call for revolution. Most Russian Socialists were pacifically inclined, reluctant to support their country, nor were they convinced that war would necessarily facilitate revolution and the downfall of the regime. Lenin refused to be hidebound by dogma. His stand was simply determined by his perception that war would aid revolution. He openly supported a Japanese victory on the grounds that Japanese capitalists were inflicting a blow against reactionary tsarist Russia, and since it was necessary to take sides, the Bolsheviks should become involved and translate an imperialist war into civil war.

Lenin shocked many on the left by his pronouncements. Nevertheless, his contempt for German Socialists who supported their Government on the outbreak of European war ten years later only showed his consistency in this respect: in 1904, as in 1914, Lenin insisted that class interests should come before national ones. The War was to be seized upon as a catalyst for revolution, and if in the process it meant the defeat of the Russian Government, that was a prospect which Lenin could view with perfect equanimity.

Points to consider

1) **Why did Lenin become a Marxist?**
2) **To what extent did Lenin adapt Marx's ideas to Russian conditions?**
3) **What qualities as a thinker and an organiser did Lenin display before 1904?**

WAITING AND HOPING, 1904–16

THE 1905 REVOLUTION

The 1905 Revolution in Russia was not a coup d'état but a series of incidents which revealed underlying discontent in several sections of Russian society, a discontent brought to a head by news of Russian defeats at the hands of the Japanese. The massacre of St Petersburg workers outside the Winter Palace on Bloody Sunday, the mutiny of the *Potemkin*, the creation of workers' councils or soviets, agitation by peasants and nationalist minorities in parts of the Empire – together they posed a serious threat to the rule of Nicholas II.

Lenin returned to Russia from Switzerland in November 1905, when the Revolution was well under way. Others had been active during his absence. Mensheviks in St Petersburg had secured the election of a soviet, with Trotsky as one of the first vice-chairmen. A general strike had broken out. The Tsar had issued a manifesto promising political and economic reforms.

Lenin quickly assessed the situation. Ever the opportunist, upon hearing of the first disturbances in 1905, he had declared that a dictatorship of workers and peasants could be achieved immediately. He had secured the support of the Bolsheviks in London for his programme of armed insurrection. He now urged action, not talk:

> Go to the youth. Organise at once and everywhere fighting brigades among students, and particularly among workers. Let them arm themselves immediately with whatever weapons they can obtain – a knife, a revolver, a kerosene-soaked rag for setting fires.
>
> Do not demand obligatory entry into the Social Democratic Party. For Christ's sake, throw out all your schemes, consign

all functions, rights, and privileges to the devil. If the Fighting Organisation does not have at least two hundred to three hundred squads in Petersburg in one to two months, then it is a dead committee and should be buried. Let the squads begin to train for immediate operations. Some can undertake to assassinate a spy or blow up a police station, others can attack a bank to expropriate funds for an insurrection. Let every squad learn, if only by beating up police. The dozens of sacrifices will be repaid with interest by producing hundreds of experienced fighters who will lead hundreds of thousands tomorrow.

Lenin argued for a close alliance between workers and peasants, behind the leadership of all the Socialist Parties. Plekhanov complained that Lenin was acting opportunistically and abandoning the idea of a two-stage revolution, a bourgeois stage followed by a Socialist stage. Lenin ingeniously argued that a revolutionary dictatorship would in fact promote capitalism, and only at a future date would the Marxists seize power and bring about Socialism.

Upon his arrival in St Petersburg, Lenin was unhappy that the Soviet, having been organised by Mensheviks and Social Revolutionaries, would serve as a rival to the Bolsheviks. However, he soon changed his view, seeing it instead as the basis of a revolutionary provisional government. But the legitimate Government had already begun its counter-offensive, and the anti-Government forces were divided. An armed rising in Moscow was crushed.

The Lessons of 1905

Lenin took the precaution of leaving St Petersburg and crossing the frontier into Finland. He defended the failed Revolution, claiming it was a dress rehearsal for a future occasion, although he also declared afterwards that a Socialist revolution was not imminent in Russia. It would take place first in Britain or France. Russia must go through a bourgeois revolution in order that the last vestiges of feudalism be destroyed, and to enable the development of capitalism and with it a strong working class. In a short book called *Two Tactics of Social Democracy in the Democratic Revolution*, published in 1905, Lenin declared:

> To claim that Russia could skip the period of capitalist development was sheer nonsense. Marxism had forever shaken itself loose from the nonsensical patter of the Populists and the anarchists to the effect that Russia can escape a capitalist development . . . The broader, the more decisive and consistent the bourgeois revolution the more certain the struggle of the proletariat against the bourgeoisie for Socialism.

Thus was Lenin able to explain away the disappointment of 1905, and, equally important for himself, to provide a theoretical justification for what to many radicals might have seemed a disaster. He certainly refused to be dispirited himself by that disappointment. Instead, Lenin sought to turn the minority position of the Bolsheviks into a strength. Dismissive of the tendency of some Mensheviks after 1905 to become involved in 'reformism', accommodating themselves to the regime, Lenin taught the Bolsheviks that by building up their Party cadres, they would be in prime position to exploit future revolutionary conditions. This was, according to Lenin, a more important and feasible task than attempting to win widespread support amongst the working class. It was not, however, an attitude that endeared Lenin to all his colleagues.

The Tsar fulfilled a promise made during the Revolution when he permitted elections to a State Duma or Parliament. However, Lenin regarded this institution as sham – and, indeed, Nicholas II was careful to reiterate his belief in his own autocratic power – and Lenin tried to persuade Socialist Parties to boycott the elections. Before the first Duma met, there was an attempt at reconciliation in Stockholm between Bolsheviks and Mensheviks. But any reconciliation had to be on Lenin's terms. He failed to achieve this. Elections to a new Central Committee of the Social Democratic Party returned a Menshevik majority. Lenin complied with the decision outwardly, but secretly he maintained his own Bolshevik clique of close supporters.

Lenin was firmly convinced of his indispensability to the Socialist movement. There was some talk of him standing for election as a Duma deputy. Yet his self-confidence and utter conviction that he was always right created problems. One of Lenin's most successful tactics with truculent colleagues was to denigrate them and split them. The Central Committee grew so wearisome of this tactic that it launched an official investigation into his behaviour in 1907. Characteristically, Lenin was unabashed. Nevertheless, long internecine struggles within Social Democratic ranks took their toll of Lenin. Whilst in Finland he fell ill. To escape the attentions of the police, Lenin and Krupskaya crossed the frontier into Sweden, in December 1907.

FOREIGN EXILE

The years between 1907 and 1914 were difficult ones for Lenin and his comrades. Prospects for revolution in Russia seemed poor; it was difficult to sustain enthusiasm amongst Party members; and funds were low. Lenin tried to interpret the trends in post-revolutionary Russia. He now urged his colleagues in Russia to participate in elections to the Third Duma in 1907, whilst also organising illegal activities such as bank raids to boost Party funds – or rather they were organised on Lenin's behalf by shadier characters like Stalin in the Caucasus. Criticism of such activities was dismissed by Lenin as bourgeois sentimentality. The ends justified the means. But it was difficult to maintain the faith, particularly as, within Russia, order was restored by Prime Minister Stolypin, who combined ruthlessness with judicious reform. Lenin believed that Stolypin's initial success was putting back the prospect of revolution, but his own response was simply to attack those Socialist colleagues with whom he disagreed all the more strongly.

Restless, Lenin drifted from Switzerland to Paris in 1909. Meanwhile, the police made inroads into the revolutionary movement inside Russia. Many comrades were arrested. Many Mensheviks put their faith in the trade union movement to better the workers' lot, and refused to be reconciled to Lenin, who still expected everything on his own terms. Lenin's influence within Russia was weakened by an understandable insistence by Bolsheviks inside Russia that they be allowed to take operational decisions without necessarily seeking guidance from Bolshevik leaders in exile.

Lenin retained strong memories of the 1905 St Petersburg Soviet. This had much more potential for him than trade unions. The basis of the Soviet-elected workers and soldiers-made it very different also from the Western-style parliamentary institutions of which Lenin was so contemptuous. He believed the soviets could combine legislative and executive functions. He had none of the mystical Western Liberal reverence for 'separation of powers', and, said Lenin, the soviets could act as the channel by which ordinary workers could join in debate and government. Ironically, the role of soviets as organs of grass-roots democracy, the dream of many Bolsheviks before the October Revolution, was to be already well in decline before Lenin's death in 1924.

Rumours later developed that whilst in exile, Lenin took solace in a string of mistresses, including a certain Elizabeth K., and Inessa Armand. There is little hard evidence of the truth of these rumours, although there has been much speculation about Armand. She was converted to Bolshevism after reading *What is to be Done?*, and met Lenin for the first time in 1911. The following year she did live with Lenin and Krupskaya, who tolerated the domestic relationship phlegmatically. Lenin was not disturbed by the rumours about his private life, but then he showed little concern about the private lives of colleagues, provided that he approved of their political stance.

Whatever the truth or otherwise of the rumours, Lenin never allowed personal indulgence to interfere seriously with his revolutionary vocation. He continued his massive output of writings, including a substantial volume called *Materialism and Empiro-Criticism*, published in 1909. This book further expounded Lenin's concept of Marxism, and contained an attack upon religion. `

OPPOSITION AND THE PRAGUE CONFERENCE

Lenin had other pressing concerns. Although there had been attempts in 1906 and 1907 to reconcile the Bolshevik and Menshevik factions, Lenin took the opposite line of asserting Bolshevik independence. However, he could not prevent some of his colleagues from maintaining contacts with Mensheviks, and even forging new links with them in 1910. At this time Lenin was isolated, with little influence over colleagues in Russia. The Central Committee tried to curb what it regarded as Lenin's factionalism. His response was to start a new Bolshevik newspaper called *The Workers' Newspaper*, in October 1910, in which Socialist opponents of Lenin were heartily attacked for their deviancy from Marx. Lenin jealousy regarded himself as the one true interpreter of Marx, although Marx, just like Lenin, never left behind him an entirely consistent canon of political and economic philosophy. Lenin could be quite abusive towards those who dissented from his views. Trotsky, for example, he labelled as 'Little Judas'. Therefore, despite his growing reputation as a theorist, it was his bitter Party in-fighting for which Lenin was most known, and for which he was increasingly criticised. However, few doubted his sincerity, and the determination which he displayed during most of these difficult years was a quality of leadership which to some extent compensated for the divisiveness for which he was also notorious.

Lenin was aware that growing labour unrest inside Russia offered opportunities to the Bolsheviks, and so he continued to agitate for a tightly-knit Party to seize the initiative. In 1910 there were probably 10,000 Marxists in Russia, divided into various factions, but Lenin repeated his argument that a small, well-organised élite could exert an influence over the proletariat out of all proportion to its size. His concern to establish the credentials of his own faction led him to focus his literary energies on matters of Party organisation and theory, and he wrote little about the actual lives of the workers and peasants inside Russia whose cause he was championing. He was more concerned with the dream of revolution than analysing the social and economic condition of his homeland, although he did comment on some of the measures taken by the tsarist regime in the years following the 1905 Revolution.

In 1912 the Sixth Party Conference was held in Prague. This was an attempt by Lenin to reinforce his authority over the Party machine, since the majority of the 18 delegates were Bolsheviks who followed his line. Nevertheless, the delegates claimed to represent the whole Social Democratic Party. Although the Congress was stage-managed, there were still complaints about Lenin's spoiling tactics in exile, and the fact that he devoted little attention to the concerns of ordinary workers inside Russia. Lenin responded by changing his earlier stance on such matters, now arguing that the Party should devote attention to the role of trade unions and other means of ameliorating the ordinary Russian's lot.

The Prague Conference was very important in Lenin's career. It, rather than 1903, marked the real birth of the Bolshevik Party. Lenin was claiming that his faction represented the Social Democratic Party, and fellow-Bolsheviks comprised the new Central Committee. Lenin and Zinoviev were the only emigré members of the Committee, and other members were prepared to argue with Lenin. But Lenin continued his disruptive tactics and his claim to authority within the movement, and it was clear that the split between the Bolsheviks and the Mensheviks was becoming final, at least at the formal level. Lenin did not appear to care, so long as he was in control of his faction.

Meanwhile, life in exile went on. Lenin and Krupskaya continued to live in rented rooms, relying on Party donations, royalties from Lenin's writings and gifts from his mother to survive. Not that Lenin lived in discomfort. And appearances were very important to Lenin. It was only when more famous that he took to wearing his 'Lenin cap'. At this stage in his career, like other self-respecting revolutionaries, he dressed in a suit and Homburg hat.

Lenin's hopes of a revival of Bolshevik fortunes in Russia were raised by the Lena goldfields strike and massacre in 1912. The event prompted Lenin to move closer to home, to Galicia. He poured out articles in *Pravda*, attacking both the Mensheviks and the Russian Government. Internal dissensions in the Party raged interminably. Bolsheviks inside Russia complained that Lenin was not doing enough constructively to help their cause. *Pravda* was full of articles by Lenin, but his theories and tactics did not strike a sympathetic chord with the workers whom Bolshevik activists inside Russia were trying to recruit. The Party was struggling to win support and to resist the inroads of the secret police.

During 1913 and 1914 Lenin was not idle. He devoted considerable study to the issue of the nationalities within the Russian Empire. What should Bolshevik policy be? Lenin openly espoused the principle of self-determination. The nationalities had the right to secede, although in practice Lenin assumed that non-Russians would not exercise this right, preferring to stay united with a workers' regime in post-revolutionary Russia. Lenin was not consistent in his views. Even before the Revolution, he occasionally asserted that secession might be refused if it were not in the interests of the working class of that nation. The solution would not be to create a federal state, but to encourage the nationalities to 'fuse' in a way which would make national differences irrelevant. This was a naive view, and it was a portent of the later Stalinist policy of Russification, which had disastrous effects upon the non-Russian nationalities. This is not to say that Lenin would have approved of Stalin's methods, but it does indicate his incapacity sometimes to think through the implications of his theories.

The Bolshevik Central Committee planned a new Congress in Cracow for the summer of 1914. Lenin was still determined that his faction should prevail, and worked to influence the selection of delegates to the

Congress and to exaggerate the degree of Bolshevik support amongst the Russian proletariat. Yet privately the truth was known. Despite an increase in labour unrest during Russia in 1914, the Bolshevik Party organisation was weak, and many of the most able Party activists were under arrest. Contacts with the emigrés were difficult. Lenin was so pre-occupied with organisational concerns that he appeared to show little interest in the explosion in the Balkans and the succeeding diplomatic crisis in Europe in the summer of 1914. And yet it was to be the general European war which, through bringing new horrors to Russia, presented new opportunities to Lenin to make his mark on the Russian and world stage.

WAR AND INTERNAL CONFLICTS

Lenin optimistically assumed that, once war had broken out, the workers of Europe would rebel against their governments. He was to be disappointed by the reaction of the Socialist Parties of western Europe, which condemned the manoeuvres leading to war, but, once war was declared, dropped opposition to their governments. Lenin was to come back to this problem in 1916 in *Imperialism, the Highest Stage of Capitalism*. But, in 1914, Lenin's concerns were more personal. Soon after the outbreak of war he was arrested by the Austrian authorities as a suspect alien, in possession of a pistol and given to walking in the mountains near the border. When it was realised that Lenin, as an anti-tsarist agitator, was more useful outside prison than within, he was released on 19 August to travel to Switzerland.

In spite of, indeed partly because of, the outbreak of war, ideological differences continued to excite the emigrés. Russian and German Socialists argued about why the war had occurred, why Socialist Parties had behaved in the way they had, and what their future strategy should be. Upon hearing the news that the German Socialists had voted in support of war credits for their government, Lenin declared: 'From today I shall cease being a social-democrat and shall become a communist!' Lenin argued forcibly: 'Turn the imperialist war into civil war'. Others were more cautious. Plekhanov, for example, supported the Allied cause on the grounds that a German victory would entail horrendous consequences for Russia, including the Russian proletariat. Lenin, in contrast, claimed that the victory of German 'kaiserism' would be a lesser evil than the victory of tsarism. This went further than most Russian Socialists, including many Bolsheviks, were prepared to go. Lenin also attacked those he accused of pacifism, and urged Bolsheviks back home to turn war against Germany into civil war. His urging was optimistic, given that there was initially widespread support inside Russia for the Government's stance against Germany.

Life in Switzerland was extremely frustrating for Lenin. Organisation amongst the emigrés was now virtually non-existent, and it was difficult even to communicate with Bolsheviks inside Russia. Lenin rebuilt an emigré organisation inside Switzerland and then devoted himself to theorising about the future. He declared that Socialism was now even more a European issue than a Russian one, and its introduction was now an immediate possibility. This conviction made Lenin even more impatient with those Socialists, or 'Social-Chauvinists' as Lenin preferred to call them, who in his view did not pursue the correct strategy. His views were put forward in two pamphlets published in 1915. *The Collapse of the Second International* and *Socialism and War*, the latter co-authored by Zinoviev. Lenin's objective was to found a Third International, in an attempt to unite all right-thinking European Socialists. Lenin's arguments were also publicised in a newspaper *Social-Democrat* and a journal *Kommunist*.

Lenin and Zinoviev attended a conference of anti-war Socialists at Zimmerwald in September 1915. Lenin condemned the existing Second International for failing to act against the war. He called for a new revolutionary International, a call which came to fruition with the creation of the Communist International after the October Revolution. The Conference condemned the war as imperialist, but little positive was achieved.

Lenin continued to be pre-occupied with disputes amongst the Bolsheviks. Perhaps this was why he commented so little upon the human side of the war, such as the effects upon soldiers and civilians, preferring instead to argue with fellow Socialists who disagreed with his political and economic theories. He argued even with close colleagues such as Zinoviev and Bukharin.

In January 1916 Lenin and Krupskaya moved from Berne to Zurich. Life was difficult. Later that year he wrote:

As regards myself personally, I will say that I need to earn. Otherwise we shall simply die of hunger, really and truly! The cost of living is devilishly high, and there is nothing to live on.

Later still he wrote to his sister Maria that 'the cost of living makes one despair and I have desperately little capacity for work because of my shattered nerves.' In addition to a shortage of funds, communication with Russia was difficult. Life for the emigrés in their small circle was claustrophobic. Yet all the while Lenin was still considering the possibility of revolution in Russia, and indeed beyond:

To the question, 'What would the party of the proletariat do if the revolution placed it in power in the present war?' we answer: 'We would propose peace to all the belligerents, the liberation of all colonies and all dependencies, all the oppressed, and those peoples who do not have equal rights . . . And we would also raise in rebellion the Socialist proletariat of Europe against their governments.

In April 1916 the Socialist Committee set up at the Zimmerwald Conference summoned another Swiss Conference, at which Lenin criticised all Socialists, Russian and others, who did not share his views on war and revolution. But his tendency to argue with all and sundry left him isolated. He had few friends among the emigrés. Lenin's ability to provoke discord was further demonstrated by his involvement in the Swiss Socialist movement. He succeeded in splitting the latter by forming a faction dedicated to organising international revolution – a faction which was to be the kernel of the Swiss Communist Party.

IMPERIALISM AND CAPITALISM

Frustrated at his inability to reach a wider audience, Lenin devoted much of his effort to writing. Between January and June 1916 he researched and wrote *Imperialism: The Highest Stage of Capitalism*. This book took Marxist analysis beyond the sphere of national capitalism into that of international capitalist competition. As Marx had once analysed nineteenth-century capitalism, Lenin tackled contemporary imperialism. The work was not wholly original, and indeed Lenin acknowledged his debt to earlier authors like Hobson and his own younger colleague Bukharin. However, Lenin's work was intended as much as a political manifesto as a dispassionate socio-economic analysis.

Lenin argued that the war was the result of capitalist states clashing with each other in their drive for new colonies and overseas markets. The capitalist countries had divided the world into colonies and semi-colonies. The latter included countries like Russia which were politically independent, but which had been infiltrated economically by capitalist powers. It was impossible for a native middle class to develop in these semi-colonies, which made the role of the proletariat, through its mouthpiece, the Party, even more crucial as the vanguard of revolution. Lenin was also confident of the revolutionary potential waiting to be tapped in what we would today call the 'Third World'. He claimed that over half the world's population lived under colonial exploitation. Wars of national liberation in countries like India or China could coincide with proletarian revolutions in capitalist countries to overthrow imperialist and capitalist rule everywhere.

The kernel of Lenin's argument was that the activities of imperialist powers carried the seeds of capitalism's destruction within them. Nations fighting imperialist wars would have to arm their workers in order to provide the necessary cannon fodder, but an armed proletariat could be made to turn its weapons against the bourgeoisie. International conflicts would dissolve into civil or class wars, from which the proletariat would, emerge triumphant. Lenin's analysis of the progress of imperialism had some relevance, even when simplistically expressed, although the pattern of events did not unfold as the logic of his argument might have suggested; after all, had the war been principally about markets and the clash of competing imperialist powers, one might have expected Britain and France, colonial rivals in the late nineteenth century, to have been on opposite sides rather than allies. However, Lenin was concerned above all to draw lessons for Russia. Russia, for Lenin, could play a crucial role in the whole scenario. When the overproducing capitalist countries, desperate for new markets, rushed into war, Russia would provide a weak link in the chain. By losing the war, the Russian experience might stimulate a proletarian takeover everywhere. Hence Lenin's contempt for patriots prepared to fight for their country rather than see that the class struggle was the real issue at stake. National governments undoubtedly would have been concerned had the attitudes of Lenin been more widespread than they were even in the depths of an apparently interminable and bloody war.

→Throughout the war Lenin was convinced that Russia was ripe for revolution. Consequently his ideas on the nature of the transitional period from semi-capitalism to fully-developed capitalism and then Socialism were changing. He was developing the idea that Russia could move very quickly into the Socialist stage of development, an idea which he wrote about more fully after the February Revolution.

However, the time for theorising was drawing to a close. Russia's political and economic problems, magnified by the disasters of war, were building up to crisis proportions. Yet the Revolution, when it came, was not brought about by Lenin or any revolutionary group. Lenin's achievement was to utilize his vision, audacity and single-minded determination to seize opportunities which were to elevate him in the space of months from being a largely unknown conspirator in exile to becoming the head of the first Marxist government in the world.

timeline	1905	First Russian Revolution
	November	Lenin arrived in St Petersburg
	1907 January	Lenin moved to Finland
	1912 January	Prague Congress. Bolsheviks effectively a separate Party
	1914	Outbreak of First World War
		Lenin moved to Switzerland

Points to consider

1) What was Lenin's role in the 1905 Revolution and what lessons did he draw from it?
2) How did Lenin's political views develop between 1905 and 1914?
3) Critically examine Lenin's interpretation of the causes of the First World War. What opportunities did he expect the war to provide for revolution and Socialism?

3

'WE WILL TURN RUSSIA UPSIDE DOWN!' – FEBRUARY TO OCTOBER 1917

THE FEBRUARY REVOLUTION

Revolution in Russia was the result of an accumulation of social, political and economic problems caused by, or magnified by, the war. Any chance that the old regime could avert a major crisis was dashed by the inability of a weak but stubborn Nicholas II to compromise his belief in divine right absolutism. Even Conservatives lost faith in a regime which had allowed Rasputin and the Empress to hold political sway whilst the Tsar was at the Front in a vain attempt to turn the tide of war in Russia's favour. Strikes and disturbances in Petrograd (the wartime name of the capital St Petersburg) in February 1917 resulted in the abdication of the Tsar and the formation of a Provisional Government, composed largely of the more liberal members of the Duma. A Soviet, elected from the ranks of workers and soldiers, and resurrecting the tradition of 1905, emerged as a rival to this Government. Despite the confusion and uncertainties, optimism was rife. Civil and political liberties were proclaimed, and liberals set about creating the freest and most democratic society in Europe.

What of the revolutionary parties themselves? They were virtually overtaken by events. The newly-formed Petrograd Soviet elected an Executive Committee, which contained independents and members of political groups, including Bolsheviks. There were some Bolsheviks in the capital, and others were soon to arrive, such as Molotov and Stalin, but many of the more prominent Bolsheviks were abroad and powerless. They had very few remaining links with Russia. Lenin's own initial surprise at the news from Petrograd was quickly translated into feverish attempts to return home and catch up with the Revolution.

LENIN AND THE FEBRUARY REVOLUTION

As a frustrated revolutionary, Lenin was naturally keen to get in on the action, particularly since the dramatic events, though long predicted by him, had finally arrived like a bolt from the blue. But Lenin also had other concerns. Could other Bolsheviks be trusted to take advantage of the new situation in which Russia found itself? There were many factions in Russia, even within his own Party. Could they lead Russia to Socialism? Lenin was suspicious from the start of the Kadets and other Liberals who were prominent in the new Government, and consequently he argued that the Bolsheviks should retain the core of their leadership in the Petrograd underground. The dangers were soon apparent to Lenin. Some Bolsheviks arriving in Petrograd, like Stalin, Sverdlov and Kamenev, were caught up in the enthusiasm of the moment, and welcomed the drift of events. And yet Molotov was already attacking the new Provisional Government. Clearly any attempt to present the Bolsheviks as a united group with a single coherent strategy would be false. Lenin was as aware of this as anybody. He needed to be on the spot.

Stalin and Kamenev took over the editorship of *Pravda* in March, and called for support of the Provisional Government and co-operation with other Parties of the Left, in return for a promise of reform. By subscribing to conditional support of the Provisional Government, Bolshevik policies appeared indistinguishable from those of the Mensheviks and the Socialist Revolutionaries. Stalin even advocated a continuation of the war as long as the German Army remained in the field. This directly contradicted Lenin's call for an end to the war and an assault on the 'bourgeois' Provisional Government.

Lenin quickly took the offensive in an attempt to establish a Bolshevik position directly at odds with that of other Parties of the Left. An article written in Zurich, but published in *Pravda* in early April, analysed the February Revolution in terms of a plot by the Allied Governments to propel members of the Provisional Government into power in order to secure Russia's continued participation in the war and to pursue their own imperialist aims. Early in April Lenin wrote *The Tasks of the Proletariat in our Revolution*. This was a strong criticism of the course of events since February. Although the Revolution had drawn millions of Russians into politics for the first time

> A gigantic petty-bourgeois wave has swept over everything and overwhelmed the class-conscious proletariat, not only by force of numbers but also ideologically; that is, it has infected and imbued very wide circles of workers with the petty-bourgeois political outlook.

This was a continuation of Lenin's theme in his five *Letters from Afar* written during March, and calling explicitly for a second revolution: 'Only a proletarian republic, backed by the rural workers and the poorest section of the peasants and town dwellers, can secure peace, provide bread, order and freedom.' The bourgeois State must be smashed, and the police, army and bureaucracy merged with the 'entire armed people'. The war would be halted and the promise of liberation offered to the oppressed of the world. Then the proletariat would take steps to achieve the transition to Socialism.

Lenin was now explicitly urging the Bolsheviks to move from 'the first to the second stage of the revolution.' This apparent abandoning of the orthodox Marxist concept of a significant gap between the two stages was too strong for the editors of *Pravda* to stomach, and they printed very little of the Letters. No wonder that Lenin was frustrated. The argument between Lenin and his colleagues was well under way before he returned to Petrograd in April.

THE RETURN TO THE FINLAND STATION

Lenin's diatribes against the Provisional Government and the war continued, but his principal concern was to return home. The Allied Governments had no reason to facilitate his passage across war-torn Europe, since the Provisional Government continued to be their ally. An idea of Lenin's to return home pretending to be a blind, deaf and dumb Swede was wisely abandoned. However, the Germans came to Lenin's rescue. They saw advantages in assisting Lenin. It is commonly assumed that the German Government's decision to provide Lenin with a 'sealed train' arose from a machiavellian plot to unleash an anti-war virus upon Russia. In fact, the original motive was more prosaic: returning Russian exiles could be exchanged for German prisoners of war held in Russia. Nevertheless, many German generals, including Ludendorff, did realise Lenin's potential as an agent of disintegration inside the Russian army.

The negotiations for Lenin's return were complex and several individuals were involved. The German Government promised no interference and did not even check the names of the travellers. The end result was that Lenin, Krupskaya, Inessa Armand, Zinoviev, Radek, 20 Bolsheviks in all, along with 12 non-Bolsheviks, boarded the train in Zurich. The returning exiles occupied one carriage, and despite the crowding, Lenin and Krupskaya were given a compartment to themselves. As usual, Lenin banned smoking anywhere near him and this caused great discomfiture to several of his colleagues. Upon reaching Stockholm, Radek persuaded Lenin to buy new boots and a pair of trousers. Lenin was less concerned with his appearance than with preparing his arguments against those colleagues in Russia who were supporting the Provisional Government.

The journey was unwelcome to many European Socialists who were suspicious of Lenin's connections with the Imperial German Government. To Lenin, the opportunity to direct the Revolution in person was the only consideration. Again, the end justified any means.

Lenin travelled from Sweden to Finland, from thence to Russia, and finally arrived at the Finland Station in Petrograd on 16 April 1917. He had been absent from Russia for ten years. He was met by a large and enthusiastic crowd. Lenin seized the stage immediately, proclaiming from the top of an armoured car to the assembled ranks of revolutionaries:

> Dear comrades, soldiers, sailors, and workers, I am happy to greet you in the name of the victorious Russian Revolution, to greet you as the vanguard of the international proletarian army.

Lenin went on to the Bolshevik headquarters and spoke there. An observer, Sukhanov, reported Lenin as speaking for about two hours, his speech containing an 'astonishing wealth of vocabulary, the whole dazzling cascade of definitions, nuances, and parallel ideas, which can be attained only through fundamental brain-work'. Lenin thundered against the war and its supporters, ending with a declaration that

A Bolshevik painting showing Lenin's arrival at the Finland Station in April 1917

Contemporary Socialism was the enemy of the international proletariat. And the very name of Social Democracy had been desecrated by treason. It was impossible to have anything in common with it, impossible to purge it: it had to be cast aside as the symbol of the betrayal of the working class'.

(N. Sukhanov, *The Russian Revolution* (1922))

At the Tauride Palace Lenin continued his calls for revolution, but he was dismissed as a madman by many Mensheviks, and even many Bolsheviks were not convinced.

Response to Lenin's return has been shrouded in the fog of myth and Soviet hagiography. Some reports speak of a charismatic performance by Lenin, that impressed even the Bolsheviks lashed by Lenin's tongue. Other evidence suggests considerable hostility to Lenin from elements on the Left, including ordinary servicemen and workers, upset that Lenin had accepted German help. There were demonstrations against Lenin. Some Socialists accused him of preaching anarchism. Opinions about Lenin varied. A Menshevik newspaper published early in April declared:

> After his speech, we can say that each significant success of Lenin will be a success of reaction, and all struggle against counter-revolutionary hopes and intrigues will be hopeless until we render politically harmless, the current which Lenin heads . . . It is imperative, by active struggle and propaganda, to render the revolution safe from this stab in the back which is being prepared for it . . . Before it is too late, Lenin and his supporters, must be given a most decisive rebuff.

In contrast, the Socialist Revolutionary leader Chernov felt that all sense of proportion had been lost:

> The average man is always inclined to expect all sorts of horrors . . . An antiChrist has now appeared. This antiChrist is Lenin. Avid for sensation, some popular newspapers reflected

Lenin in disguise in the summer of 1917

the panic of the average man, others exploited it in the interests of sales . . .

Lenin can only thank his enemies for this attention . . . It is in the interests of Lenin to become a 'bugaboo' to the bourgeoisie, to play upon its imagination as a living embodiment of the spectre of social war with an arsonists's torch in hand. He can only rejoice at the hatred of the bourgeoisie, to have daily all the mongrels, foaming at the mouth, rush at him through the literary back door . . .

Lenin is unquestionably a pure man, and all filthy insinuation of the narrow-minded press to German money in connection with his passing through Germany must be kicked aside with disgust. But he is a man with a deadened moral sensitivity. He marches toward his chief aim. All that is important for him is the correctness of the basic direction . . .

Lenin has a great militant temperament and a tremendous reserve of energy. But . . . his settling of accounts with opponents screeches crunchingly like iron over glass. His is a sort of uncouth socialism, for Lenin employs a clumsy axe where a fine scalpel is called for.

(The SR newspaper, *Delo Naroda* 16 April 1917)

Clearly, Lenin's return to Russia was significant. Sukhanov called Lenin 'an unusually happy combination of theoretician and popular leader'. He was a genius, albeit a narrow-minded one. He was indispensable to the Party: 'There could be neither independent thinking nor organisational base in the Bolshevik Party without Lenin'. Lenin's radicalism and 'primitive demagogy, unrestrained either by science or common sense' forced ordinary Party members to choose an alternative: 'either keep the old principles of Social Democracy and Marxist science, but without Lenin, without the masses, and without the Party; or stay with Lenin and the Party and conquer the masses together in an easy way, having thrown overboard the obscure, unfamiliar Marxist principles'.

Sukhanov was writing after the Revolution, and was unfair in implying that Lenin chose the easy path to popularity. That was not an obvious path in April 1917. The real significance of Lenin's return was that Russia was in a state of instability, with both civilians and soldiers enjoying the heady experience of freedom but also suffering privations and being uncertain of their course of action. Lenin acted decisively in these circumstances, and seized every opportunity to promote his beliefs. Many members of the Provisional Government believed that Lenin's return was of minor importance, but its future leader, Kerensky, showed more foresight. Kerensky remarked that his arrival meant that the Revolution was about to 'really start'.

THE APRIL THESES

Lenin could not persuade most of his prominent colleagues of the correctness of his views and tactics. Nevertheless, he went ahead and published his famous *April Theses* in *Pravda*. The Theses had been prepared during the train journey home. The text was short, but it was the most significant work produced by Lenin during his career. The work was forceful and propagandist, stronger on tactics than Marxist theory.

Lenin reiterated his attacks on the 'imperialist war', and he urged a revolt against the Provisional Government and the transfer of power to the soviets. He did not explain why Russia, which he accepted was at an early stage of capitalist development, was now ready for Socialist revolution. Lenin was ready for action, and it was easier to seize the opportunity to act and to construct a suitable theory later.

After a new revolution, continued Lenin, a Soviet Government would introduce practical reforms in order to prepare the ground for Socialism. The new Government would be based upon the workers' soviets, not a parliament. It was necessary to enlighten the masses as to where their true interests lay: hence the importance of propaganda against the Provisional Government. Whereas some on the Left were sitting back and admiring the achievements of February, Lenin saw the revolution as a dynamic, continuing process. The soviets were already in existence, and therefore power should be transferred to them from the bourgeois Provisional Government. The soviets themselves must be cleansed of opportunists and reformists, in order that they become genuine organs of revolutionary power.

Before 1917, Lenin had expected there to be a substantial interval between the bourgeois and socialist revolutions, taken up by a period of capitalist development. Now he was calling for 'uninterrupted revolution': why wait for power if it could be seized now? Lenin accepted that the concept of revolution in two distinct stages, more orthodoxly Marxist, was correct in giving a 'scientific' basis to policy. However, Lenin the man of action could also argue that in 'real life' it might be advisable or necessary to adopt specific tactics which might not sit easily with the theory. Lenin wrote that such a peculiar situation existed in Russia with 'Dual Power' between the Provisional Government and the Petrograd Soviet.

⟶ The April Theses were not a blueprint for the post-revolutionary State. Although there were statements about the nationalisation of land and control of banking, there was nothing on the organisation of industry. However, the importance of the document lies in its directness and the fact that the Bolsheviks were for the first time since February presented with a clear alternative to the policies pursued by Stalin and Kamenev.

Soviet historiography, and some Western writing, have given the impression that Lenin's clarion call for revolution immediately stimulated the Bolsheviks into adopting a new course of action. In reality, many prominent Bolsheviks were openly hostile. For example, Kamenev opposed Lenin in *Pravda*, which published an article condemning Lenin's idea of uninterrupted revolution as 'unacceptable'.

What is true is that Lenin's relentless arguments against dissenters, in conjunction with the political horse-trading and compromise tactics indulged in by the other Socialist parties, gradually won him support from Bolsheviks at most levels. Some of the more right-wing Bolsheviks simply deserted the movement, which strengthened Lenin's hand. News that the Foreign Minister, Milyukov, had secretly promised continuing military support to the Allies, persuaded more waverers to Lenin's side. The essential programme of the April Theses was adopted by the All-Russian Bolshevik Party Conference in May, although Kamenev and some others still professed reservations.

'ALL POWER TO THE SOVIETS'
—

Lenin and his colleagues on the Central Committee continued to disagree on some issues. Although a declaration calling for peace without annexation and indemnities, and a promise of the right to national self-determination, were issued in May, the Central Committee would not publish Lenin's call for the nationalisation of land. There was also concern among some Bolsheviks at the publicity Lenin was attracting. Much of the publicity was bad, consisting of attacks by political opponents on his political and personal life, but nevertheless it was making Lenin a well-known name outside political circles for the first time. Lenin was not interested in becoming a 'personality', but some colleagues thought this to be a dangerous possibility. Lenin was emerging into the limelight, proving an effective orator in his frequent public speeches. His press output was also important in spreading awareness about himself, since he did not visit Moscow in 1917, and indeed rarely shifted outside Petrograd. His written style became more 'popular', and his articles were now probably read outside political circles for the first time.

Lenin's strategy increasingly revolved around the issue of 'All power to the soviets'. The Bolsheviks were not strong enough to seize power by themselves. But the soviets contained many representatives, both civilian and military, who were non-Bolshevik. Therefore, an uprising in the name of the Petrograd Soviet stood more chance of success than a Bolshevik coup. A cynical interpretation would be that Lenin knew this all along, and was using the Soviet only as a cover for an eventual Bolshevik dictatorship. Or perhaps he believed that the support of the majority of the proletariat was essential for a seizure of power, and this could only be achieved through a Bolshevik-led Soviet as opposed to the Bolsheviks operating as a minority group outside the Soviet.

Lenin was certainly aided by circumstances. The declaration by Foreign Minister, Milyukov, that Russia would fight on in the cause of Allied unity, was a blunder in a country sick of war. A reorganisation of the Government in May, involving the accession of some Mensheviks and Socialist Revolutionaries to the cabinet, compromised their leaders when the going got tougher. A breakdown of authority was signalled by mutinies in the Army and the seizure of land by peasants. Lenin was in tune with the popular mood and he was decisive. In a memorable speech at the All-Russian Congress of the Soviets on 16 June 1917, Lenin declared that the Bolsheviks were ready for power. Kerensky replied at the same meeting. His own opposition to Lenin was uncompromising:

> I dare say that Citizen Lenin has forgotten what Marxism is
> ... You, Bolsheviks, recommend childish solutions – 'arrest,

kill, destroy! What are you, Socialists or police of the old regime?

But Kerensky, the great orator, impressed the audience of soldiers, workers and sailors less than Lenin did.

THE JULY DAYS

However, attempts to portray Lenin's march to power as one of inexorable progress would be misleading. There were hiccoughs on the way. Late in June a demonstration against the Government was first planned, then called off. Fellow Socialists accused the Bolsheviks of a conspiracy to bring about counter-revolution. Stalin certainly supported the idea of armed demonstrations. For once Lenin was uncertain. There were doubts that the Bolsheviks could have turned a demonstration into a successful coup at this stage. Lenin faced the dilemma of any revolutionary leader: how to keep enthusing one's followers whilst dissuading them from premature and possible disastrous action. The Bolsheviks temporarily took a back seat in the Soviet and Lenin kept a low profile. Lenin uncharacteristically urged caution on the Bolsheviks: 'If we were now able to seize power, it is naive to think that having taken it we should be able to hold on to it'.

Further difficulties for the Bolsheviks were created by the July Days. Kerensky, seeking to buttress his own authority, launched a major offensive against the Germans early in July. The offensive failed, and simmering discontent on the streets of Petrograd was turned into outright revolt. The Central Committee of the Bolshevik Party held a long debate as to whether or not it should attempt to take over the leadership of the revolt. Lenin missed the debate: having complained of overwork and ill-health he travelled to Finland for a few days of rest. The Central Committee decided to support the revolt, but quickly abandoned this course when it became evident that the Government was suppressing the disturbances. Lenin, on his return to Petrograd, appealed for support but gave no clear direction. The violence in Petrograd petered out, partly because the demonstrations, ugly though they were, lacked co-ordination or leadership.

The Provisional Government seized the opportunity to reinforce its position and ordered the arrest of Lenin and other leading Bolsheviks on the charge of inciting insurrection, helped by German money. Almost certainly the charge was true. Money had been transferred from German sources to the Bolsheviks, mostly via Stockholm, although Lenin denied this. The Government could not make more capital out of the affair, since conclusive evidence was not to hand. The charges, had they been proved beyond doubt at the time, would have seriously damaged Lenin's reputation in some quarters. Equally beyond doubt is that Lenin would have justified taking German money if it helped his revolutionary cause. Any charge of disloyalty or lack of patriotism he would have dismissed as irrelevant, and therefore only in a very loose sense can Lenin be called a German agent.

Nevertheless, it did seem important in July 1917 that Lenin avoided arrest. Together with Zinoviev he went into hiding in Petrograd, and the Bolsheviks adopted a low profile again. Sukhanov was very critical of Lenin's behaviour, pointing out that Lenin's colleagues were content to serve out a few weeks in prison whilst Lenin ran for cover, and refused to answer the charges and rumours against him. But Lenin was more interested in drawing lessons from the July Days. In *Three Crises*, written on 7 July, he drew the lesson that the movement's tactics must be quickly changed:

All hopes for a peaceful development of the Russian Revolution have vanished for good. This is the objective situation: either complete victory for the military dictatorship, or victory for the workers' armed uprising.

But it was useless now to look to the soviets:

The present Soviets have failed, have suffered complete defeat, because they are dominated by the Socialist Revolutionary and Menshevik parties. At the moment these Socialists are like sheep brought to the slaughterhouse and bleating pitifully under the knife.

Lenin and Zinoviev moved into the countryside near Petrograd. Members of the Central Committee visited them to update them on events in the capital. During this self-imposed exile Lenin worked on *State and Revolution*, to be published after the Bolsheviks came to power.

Then, as the security net tightened, Lenin disguised himself and slipped across the Finnish border. He was beardless and wearing a wig. His documents declared him to be a Mr Ivanov.

CONTINUING THE ATTACK FROM FINLAND

Whilst in Finland, Lenin faced the continuing problems of persuading the Bolsheviks to accept a coherent strategy of revolution, meaning his own. This was not easy, since local Party bodies frequently ignored instructions issued by the Central Committee, and the Central Committee itself was far from convinced that Lenin was right. It was certainly dumbfounded by a pamphlet it received from Lenin on 'The Political Situation'. The pamphlet was written on 10 July, and demanded a reversal of the previous call of 'All Power to the Soviets' on the grounds that the soviets, dominated by Mensheviks, were trying to crush the Bolsheviks. Lenin now decided that Bolsheviks on factory committees would be the cornerstone of a new Socialist government. Typically, when the Central Committee rejected his arguments, Lenin simply returned to the attack, although he then compromised by explaining that the soviets might play a major role in the future when they were purged of their 'bourgeois collaboration'. Of more immediate significance for Lenin were new elections to the Central Committee, which returned a more left-wing membership, easier to persuade to his point of view.

THE KORNILOV REVOLT

The departure of Lenin from Petrograd seemed to be the nadir of Lenin's fortunes. Kerensky became Prime Minister, and many Bolsheviks, in the absence of their leader, felt that the argument that the Bolsheviks could seize power was a weak one. However, the recovery of Lenin's fortunes was to go hand in hand with the decline in the authority of the Provisional Government. Kerensky's coalition Government of 25 July contained a majority of Socialists. This eventually confirmed Lenin in his belief that the Bolsheviks should have nothing to do with other Parties, but he did briefly toy with the idea that the Mensheviks and Socialist Revolutionaries might take power through the soviets, and then the Bolsheviks would achieve power themselves by peaceful persuasion of the voters. Although an uncharacteristic stance for Lenin, it was further proof that he was not entirely consistent in his revolutionary thinking. However, he soon reverted to his more characteristic call for an uprising. By mid-September Lenin was openly calling for a seizure of power on the grounds that the Bolsheviks had won majorities in the Petrograd and Moscow Soviets. The fact that these bodies comprised only a minority of the proletariat was immaterial: the important and legitimising factor was that they represented the majority of the *politically-conscious vanguard* of the workers.

However, whilst these arguments were being aired a more immediate crisis had to be overcome. In late August the Commander-in-Chief of the Army, General Kornilov, launched an attempted coup. He sent his forces towards Petrograd with a frank declaration that 'It's time to hang the German supporters and spies, with Lenin at their head, and to disperse the Soviet of Workers' and Soldiers' Deputies so that it will never reassemble'. The Kornilov Revolt marked the breach between Kerensky's Government and the Army. Lacking the force to defend himself, Kerensky ordered the release of the Bolshevik leaders under arrest since July. If Kerensky was expecting gratitude he was mistaken. Lenin, writing on 12 September to the Central Committee, called for resistance to Kornilov, but explicitly declared that this did not mean an alliance with Kerensky. In fact it was the opposite:

> As to the talk of defence of the country, of a united front of revolutionary democracy, of supporting the Provisional Government, and so forth, we must oppose it ruthlessly as being mere *talk*. This is the time for action.

Kerensky made a final attempt to rally support with the summoning of a 'Pre-Parliament', containing representatives from the soviets, trade unions and political groupings, including the Bolsheviks. Still in Finland, Lenin demanded of the Central Committee furiously that the Bolsheviks should refuse participation. He urged revolution instead:

> Having obtained a majority in the Soviets of Workers' and Soldiers' Deputies of both capitals, the Bolsheviks can, and must, take over the power of government . . . Neither can we 'wait' for the Constituent Assembly . . . It would be naive to

wait for a 'formal' majority for the Bolsheviks; no revolution ever waits for that . . . History will not forgive us if we do not assume power now.

He continued in a letter to the Central Committee to outline the precise military measures necessary to seize key areas of Petrograd.

Lenin's arguments were exaggerated and his language fierce, but he was fighting a battle to get his way within his own Party. Lenin was in hiding and possibly not in the best position to understand the situation in Petrograd. It was probably as well for him that his colleagues in the thick of things in the capital did not launch a coup in September. At that stage it might well have failed, with disastrous consequences for Lenin and the Bolsheviks.

The Die is Cast

Lenin did acquire a great bonus. Trotsky was by now clearly on Lenin's side, and he was elected chairman of the Petrograd Soviet on 8 October. This, plus evidence of an increasingly pro-Bolshevik mood amongst the factory workers, persuaded Lenin to move closer to Petrograd. Lenin was now insisting to the Central Committee that a Bolshevik coup should not even wait for the forthcoming All-Russian Congress of Soviets to meet.

Lenin, disguised as a protestant clergyman, slipped back into Petrograd and addressed a secret meeting of the Bolshevik Central Committee on 23 October. He called for an immediate seizure of power, arguing that the moment was right, and that if the Bolsheviks did not act, Kerensky would abandon Petrograd to the advancing Germans. Lenin's arguments provoked hours of discussion. Eventually a vote in favour of armed insurrection was passed by 10 votes to 2, the two negative votes being cast by Zinoviev and Kamenev. No practical decisions were taken on the tactics of insurrection.

There were still a number of hesitant Bolsheviks outside this immediate circle, but their reservations were brushed aside. Six days later the Central Committee met again. Lenin argued that Russia faced a simple choice between a right-wing Kornilov-style dictatorship or a Bolshevik coup. Kamenev and Zinoviev disputed Lenin's claim that a majority of Russian, and indeed the world's, workers were awaiting a Bolshevik coup. They were of course technically correct, but Lenin argued that since the Bolsheviks had by now won majorities in the Petrograd and Moscow Soviets, they effectively *were* the majority of the revolutionary vanguard. This was the true meaning of 'majority', not a definition based on simple numbers.

THE OCTOBER COUP

The precise roles of Lenin and Trotsky in the October Revolution have been much debated, and have been the subject of considerable propaganda. The facts are clear. It was Trotsky who proposed the organisation of a Military Revolutionary Committee from the Petrograd Soviet, and it was this Committee which organised and led the coup d'état which seized control of the Winter Palace and key points of the capital. Lenin approved of Trotsky's proposal. There were non-Bolshevik and Bolshevik members of this Committee. Trotsky was a member, but not Lenin. The Bolshevik Central Committee approved the arrangements, recognising the propaganda value of the Soviet, rather than just the Bolshevik Party, appearing to seize power.

Just before the coup Lenin wrote to the Central Committee that power was to be seized 'not in opposition to the Soviets but on their behalf'. Lenin's role in the coup itself was not crucial. The Central Committee ordered him to stay in hiding. Eventually he made his own decision and travelled by tram to the Smolny Institute, the Bolshevik and Soviet head-quarters. As armed units of the Red Guard occupied their designated positions in Petrograd, Lenin waited in the Smolny. It was Trotsky and Sverdlov who directed most of the operations.

Eventually, after the arrest of the Provisional Government, without Kerensky, who had fled, Lenin appeared at the Second Congress of Soviets. There, after a great ovation, he announced the success of the Revolution.

Lenin spoke not of a Bolshevik victory but of the victory of Soviet power and of the imminent world Socialist revolution. Yet it had been Trotsky who had insisted that the Petrograd Soviet must authorise the coup, making it 'legal' until the Congress met. Lenin had not appreciated Trotsky's arguments, but now reaped the benefits of his actions. Power was handed to Lenin, but it was with some appearance of legality, which was important to its acceptance. The effectiveness of Bolshevik organisation can be overrated. The Bolsheviks won support chiefly because, by October, they were identified, at any rate in the cities, with Soviet power, and it was the idea of Soviet power which was becoming increasingly popular.

In his later *History* of the Revolution, Trotsky wrote of the 'chain of objective historic forces' at work in 1917, but he admitted that Lenin had been 'a great link in the chain'. In fact, Lenin's ideas on the mechanics of the coup might have proved disastrous had they been implemented. For example, Lenin had advocated that the coup be started in Moscow, where the Bolshevik organisation was weaker and the Socialist Revolutionaries had considerable support. It was Trotsky's strategy that was adopted, and his future enemy, Stalin, declared the Party's debt to Trotsky in an article written in 1918.

One danger in putting Lenin at the centre of events in 1917 is that it can lead to the assumption that he controlled the Party. The Party was not Lenin's personal instrument, nor was it a homogenous body by October 1917. Following the February Revolution there was an influx into the Bolshevik ranks of Mensheviks, Socialist Revolutionaries and previously uncommitted souls who did not gell quickly and were not all at Lenin's beck and call. And yet it is difficult to believe that the October Revolution would have broken out or developed in the way that it did without Lenin. The importance of his role was seen in the events leading up to the coup and immediately afterwards: adapting tactics when necessary, but never losing sight of the final aim of seizing power. He never allowed the opponents or doubters to sway him. It was this clarity of purpose and determination that enabled Lenin to seize power in the vacuum which developed as the Provisional Government lost control.

The Bolshevik victory was an extraordinary event. Kamenev and Zinoviev were correct in labelling Lenin's policy a gamble. Outside Petrograd and Moscow the Bolsheviks were opposed by most peasants and the core of the Army. Had the Bolshevik coup failed, a right-wing military coup would have been a distinct possibility. Even after Lenin's initial success, there was widespread speculation that his new Government would fall if only the Army or another group moved against it. Lenin's gamble did succeed – not that he regarded it as a gamble. Lenin was confident of success, and he bullied his colleagues into action. He put faith in ordinary people, and was considerably influenced by Marx's analysis of the achievements, albeit temporary, of the people of Paris during the Paris Commune of 1871.

THE THEORY AND PRACTICE OF POWER

After the October coup it was Lenin who articulated the next plan of action. This was a very necessary task since little thought had been given to the organisation of a new State beyond a few slogans. For all Trotsky's contribution to the victory, only Lenin had the political standing to force through crucial measures, and the flexibility to accept *faits accompli* when necessary, an example of the latter being the seizure of land by the peasants. Lenin himself was a master of the slogan when required, but now real policies had to be implemented. His ruthlessly pragmatic mind was to serve the Bolsheviks well, although survival in the face of a largely hostile or indifferent population was the first priority. For example, in order to survive he was quite prepared to adopt the Socialist Revolutionary programme of giving land to the peasantry.

Lenin had given some thought to the future in the months before October. *State and Revolution* had been written during this period. Lenin accepted the orthodox Marxist view of the State as an instrument of oppression wielded by the ruling economic class. Consequently, the bourgeois State must be replaced after a revolution – completely replaced, since in earlier revolutions State power had simply passed from one ruling élite to another. The police, the bureaucracy, and other organs of State repression must be abolished. All citizens would take part in government and defence. Lenin had the intellectual's contempt for administrators: ordinary people could do their jobs. Where old 'experts' had to be retained, they must at least be closely supervised.

Lenin agreed with Marx that there would be a new 'Dictatorship of the Proletariat' after the Revolution, and this would eradicate the traces of the bourgeois phase of History. This would take time: only after many years would oppression completely disappear, as the classless society emerged. The Dictatorship of the Proletariat would be based upon the soviets. This for Lenin solved the problem of how to involve the majority of the population in the running of the State, and would ensure that bureaucratic abuses of power and privilege would be prevented. This system of Government would establish Socialism. People would be paid in accordance with the amount of work done. Eventually, under Communism, social classes would disappear, along with the State, and any distinction between mental and physical work would also disappear. Lenin gave little thought to the peasantry, and skated over the dangers

A faked photograph, printed in British and French magazines in December 1917, with the caption: 'Lenin, Prime Minister of the Bolshevik regime (on the right)'.

of uniting the law-making powers and their administration in the hands of one body.

Was Lenin being naive? He assumed that because, under capitalism, many industries and services such as the railways were large-scale organisations, the task of running them had become simplified, and was within the scope of 'all literate people'. Therefore, a large-scale bureaucracy was unnecessary. He ignored the fact that large bureaucracies did develop a life and ethos of their own in advanced societies. Lenin was worldly enough to recognise that not all controls would disappear overnight, but he assumed that no large-scale repression would be necessary against enemies of the new regime. Lenin was certainly ambivalent on some key issues, and has therefore been variously accused by hostile commentators of lacking in intellectual rigour, or worse, of being hypocritical. Sometimes during 1917 he included poorer peasants in his definition of the Dictatorship of the Proletariat, at other times he did not. At times he spoke in favour of a Constituent Assembly, at other times he implied that he would not necessarily abide by any decisions made by such a body. It is not possible to find a coherent theory of the post-Leninist State in Lenin's writings during 1917, but then he was not formulating his ideas in an academic ivory tower, but in a country in the flux of war and revolution.

timeline	1917 February	Outbreak of Russian Revolution
	March	Provisional Government set up
	April	Lenin returned to Petrograd
		Lenin's *April Theses* issued
	July	July Days. Lenin fled to Finland
	August	Kornilov Rebellion
	October	Bolsheviks instigated second Revolution of the year

Points to consider

1) What was the message and significance of Lenin's *April Theses*?
2) Why were there two revolutions in Russia in 1917?
3) What factors account for the increase in Bolshevik support between February and October 1917?
4) How crucial was Lenin's role in the October Revolution?
5) Estimate the comparative strengths of Lenin as a theorist and practical politician during his career up to October 1917.

THE STRUGGLE FOR SURVIVAL AND UTOPIA

EARLY DAYS AND EARLY MEASURES

After the capture of the Winter Palace, the climax of the October Revolution, members of the Congress of Soviets protested at the actions of the Military Committee in carrying out a coup d'état. Lenin's ringing declaration that 'State power had passed into the hands of the organ of the Petrograd Soviet of Workers' and Soldiers' Deputies' did not appease its members. However, the walk-out of Mensheviks and other opponents from the Congress left the field open to the Bolsheviks and their allies, the Left Socialist Revolutionaries. Lenin, *de facto* head of a new Government, had to form an administration from nothing, in a country still at war and in a state of chaos.

Decrees were issued on several subjects. One of Lenin's first measures was a Decree on Peace, calling on all Governments to negotiate a 'just, democratic peace' without annexations or indemnities. It was a clever move by Lenin: the Decree did not repeat his earlier language which had called upon the warring peoples to rise against their own Governments. Lenin was probably deliberately echoing the American President's call for peace based on national self-determination, in the hope that Russia would avoid losing territory in any carve-up at the end of the war. If Lenin was hoping that a 'responsible' approach would win sympathy outside Russia, he was soon to be disillusioned.

The New Government

For several weeks after the Revolution the character of the new administration was very uncertain. It is doubtful that Lenin had any wish to share power with the other left-wing parties, but if this was the case he did not publicise the fact. He had first of all to persuade his colleagues on the Central Committee to his views. The very uncertainty of the situation, and the fact that nobody had thought very far ahead about the practicalities of government, probably helped Lenin. The new Government was entitled the 'Soviet of People's Commissars', (later to become SOVNARKOM), and ministerial posts were handed out almost casually. Lenin's official position was 'Chairman of the Soviet of People's Commissars'. However, his real authority derived from his leadership of the Party. A new system of 'Dual Power' was already developing: one in which responsibilities were divided between Party and Government, but with the weight of authority heavily in favour of the former. This system was to continue and develop further long after Lenin's death.

In the early months of the new regime Lenin had several pre-occupations, particularly the setting up of the new administration and passing measures designed both to protect it and to produce vast changes in the social and economic structure of the country. He still found time to write. Lenin's energy was all the more astonishing in that by temperament he found it difficult to delegate responsibility. Even so, many of the changes which took place throughout Russia were the result of local initiatives. Poor communications and pressing problems in Petrograd prevented the formation of anything approaching a centralised administration at this stage.

Peace with Germany

One of Lenin's first priorities had to be the ending of the war with Germany. Reconstruction and even survival were impossible with the Germans on Russian soil. Lenin was in something of a dilemma. He needed a breathing space in order to deal with opposition at home – in his words to 'strangle the bourgeoisie' – but he had also shown an interest in continuing the war against Germany as a 'revolutionary war', that is, a war fought on behalf of the German proletariat in the hope of making a common cause between the workers of both countries and overthrowing the German Government. Lenin's Marxism was orthodox enough to convince him that a Socialist revolution could not be sustained in one backward country alone: capitalist powers were bound to prevent it from succeeding. The Revolution must be exported. One means was to appeal to the peoples of the warring countries over the heads of their governments. Another was to be the establishment of the Communist International in Moscow in 1919. But, for the time being, Lenin the pragmatist realised the need to make what he conceded was an 'obscene peace'.

Therefore, an armistice was signed with the Germans and peace negotiations began. Lenin ordered that any German conditions should be accepted. This was too much for his negotiator, Trotsky, who at one stage broke off negotiations. Lenin had to persuade Trotsky and other unhappy comrades that concessions were not just inevitable, but that they were of only minor and temporary importance. After all, since all were convinced that revolution was about to break out in Germany, the issue of national frontiers would dissolve into irrelevance. But Lenin's arguments were practical rather than idealistic:

> Undoubtedly the peace which we are now compelled to sign is a rotten one, but if war should break out again, our government would be wiped out and peace would be made by some other government. We must become strongly entrenched in power, and for that we need time.

Lenin had great difficulty in convincing his colleagues of the need to concede to German demands, and he was faced with several resignations and closely-won votes on the Central Committee, but eventually peace was signed in March 1918. The Peace of Brest-Litovsk stripped the old Russian Empire of large chunks of territory and money. Lenin felt obliged to justify the signing for months afterwards, but he also declared privately that he would honour the terms only for as long as it was necessary. According to his secretary, Lenin refused even to read the 'impudent' terms when they were brought to him, declaring that 'I shall neither read the Treaty nor carry out its terms whenever there is a chance not to do so'.

The Constituent Assembly

Another immediate issue with which Lenin had to deal was that of the Constituent Assembly. The Provisional Government had promised to hold elections to such a legislative body throughout the months of its brief existence, but had repeatedly put off the date, given the critical military situation. Lenin had maintained that the Government never intended to allow the elections. They had in fact been fixed for 25 November. With the October Revolution having meanwhile succeeded, Lenin felt obliged to allow the election to go ahead. Lenin himself stood as a representative of the Baltic Fleet. Voting took place in December.

Lenin at his office in 1918

The results were a disappointment for the Bolsheviks. They received less than a quarter of the votes cast. The Socialist Revolutionaries won a clear majority, although their Party had meanwhile split into two wings. Lenin claimed that voters were unaware of this fact, just as he claimed that the elections were held before the Bolsheviks were widely known in most parts of Russia and before the new Government's policies had had a chance to take effect. Lenin's commentary on the results was actually quite ingenious. He pointed out that the Bolsheviks had done best in the towns; and in this epoch of history 'The town cannot be equal to the country . . . The town inevitably *leads* the country'. The Bolsheviks had the support of 'the revolutionary vanguard of the proletariat which had been steeled in the long and persevering struggle against opportunism.' (Article in *Communist International*, December 1919.)

Whatever justice there was in Lenin's claims, his response to the elections was unambiguous and extreme. Some of the newly-elected SR deputies were arrested. The Assembly met, briefly, in January. SOVNARKOM had announced that the Assembly would only be tolerated if it upheld 'soviet power'. The session of the Assembly was marked by commotion and intimidation. Lenin was present, and ordered the closing of the session. He refused to allow another session to be held. SOVNARKOM ratified Lenin's decision on 6 January, ensuring that opposition between the Bolsheviks and their political opponents would harden still further. Civil war was close. Lenin was unrepentant. He told Trotsky that the dissolution of the Assembly 'means a complete and frank liquidation of the idea of democracy by the idea of dictatorship. It will serve as a good lesson'. Later in the year Lenin dismissed the notion of democracy as a meaningful mode of expression in a country still 'under the bourgeois yoke'. In such a situation 'Only scoundrels and imbeciles can think that the proletariat must first win a majority of votes in elections'. It was more important for the proletariat, through the Party, to seize the power of the State by whatever means were necessary, and then use it to construct Socialism. Or, to put it more bluntly, the man who had only just seized power was not about to hand it over to another body as the result of democratic processes which he despised as being a relic of a passing era.

LENIN IN THE SMOLNY

Studies of the post-Revolutionary period in Russia usually focus upon the great events and political decisions. The daily pressures upon those at the centre of power can be overlooked. The period between the Revolution and March 1918, during which Lenin based himself in the Smolny in Petrograd, shows the frenetic life which the leader chose for himself, or was forced to choose.

Rising early, and retiring in the early hours of the following morning, Lenin would attend one meeting after another. Often he was responding to pressures and crises rather than initiating events himself. At the other extreme, he was often bound up in comparatively minor activities, another indication of his inability to delegate: for example, meeting ordinary petitioners, worrying about passes and ration cards for visitors to the Smolny and those who worked there. Difficulties were compounded by the lack of a properly-trained and experienced back-up staff.

Lenin received on average 300 letters a week. In addition to reading these, he listened to reports about the situation in the provinces. Lenin could communicate directly by telephone to commissars and important officials. He also frequently used the telegraph service. During this period his own serious literary output ran to several thousand words. He chaired 73 out of the 77 SOVNARKOM sessions, which often lasted well into the night. He would add to and delete from the agenda. He expected high standards of conduct, sometimes fining members who arrived late. Smoking was forbidden, to the discomfiture of some colleagues. Levity was only permitted when formal business was concluded. All decisions seem to have had Lenin's personal assent, and he wrote or amended many laws himself. SOVNARKOM set up committees to deal with particular issues, and appointed agents or special commissions to impose its authority in the provinces. Lenin frequently interfered in these matters and subordinates' decisions. Nevertheless, he was generally regarded by his staff as considerate as well as demanding, and the fact that Lenin and his colleagues drew little more than workmen's wages was widely appreciated by outsiders.

Lenin's total lack of experience as an administrator proved no handicap. The leader had boundless self-confidence. He simply threw himself into the task of directing events himself. Emotional support was provided by Krupskaya. As in the old days of foreign exile, Lenin permitted himself occasional strolls around the workers' districts of Petrograd, to the consternation of his security staff. Pleasures were few: the luxury of a small domestic staff, and an extensive library. It was a life of superior material quality to most Russians at this period, but still relatively austere.

In contrast to the incessant Government activity described above, the Central Committee of the Party met only 17 times during the period from October 1917 to March 1918. Lenin missed only two of the meetings. His practice was to allow free debate amongst colleagues, although he disliked bowing to a majority if he demurred on any particular issue. Lenin also attended some meetings of the soviets, but interfered less with their executives, usually rubber-stamping decisions.

It would be a mistake to assume that Lenin's control of political events was total. There were conflicts of outlook and policies among Bolsheviks at all levels. They rarely touched Lenin personally, because his position of authority was usually unchallenged, not by virtue of his official position, but by virtue of his achievements, his self-confidence, his reputation, and his skill at fighting his corner when he *did* feel threatened. Not even Trotsky rivalled Lenin in prestige. Soon after the Revolution, another prominent Bolshevik, Zinoviev, was already beginning a personality cult with his declaration that 'the entire Russian Revolution showed that undoubtedly comrade Lenin is the sole person of genius among us'. Lenin was a difficult man to challenge even for those who were less swayed by the growing mood of adulation. Lenin's reputation before the Revolution, at least in revolutionary circles, was that of a dogged, divisive individual, adept at splitting the opposition, fighting his corner, and sometimes winning the argument by a sheer bloody-mindedness which wore down those who disagreed. Such a veteran of political in-fighting was not going to be easily deflected from his own path once in power. Also, he learned new skills. Once an underground operator, he now proved a more than capable public orator. Yet he never lost the traits which had served him well in the old days: such as the ability to shift his ground when convenient, which now enabled him to mount appeals to both ordinary workers and intellectuals.

In this post-Revolutionary period, Lenin was comparatively neglectful of the Party. Perhaps this helps to explain why he was late in recognising trends within the Party of which he was to disapprove in his last years. However, he cannot be absolved from responsibility for such trends, particularly those which made the Party authoritarian in outlook and behaviour. Lenin himself was accessible as an individual. Those who disagreed with him in conversation were not in fear of their liberty or their lives. Yet Lenin showed no concern about human rights on a more general level. He created no checks to the development of arbitrary institutional power, and it was his refusal to accommodate the Bolsheviks with the other left-wing Parties, the Mensheviks and Socialist Revolutionaries, which prevented the real possibility of a more broadly-based Government from emerging.

REPRESSION

Consolidation of the regime had to be another of Lenin's priorities after the Revolution. Opposition to Lenin's coup came not just from natural opponents on the Right and from other left-wing Parties, but also from old Bolsheviks who could not accept Lenin's apparent disregard for Marxist theory in launching the coup, and who could not believe that the regime would last. Lenin's old friend, the respected writer Maxim Gorky, spoke for many when he criticised Lenin in a newspaper article of 21 November 1917:

> Blind fanatics and unscrupulous adventurers are rushing headlong towards 'social revolution' – as a matter of fact it is the road to anarchy, the ruin of the proletariat and the Revolution.
>
> Along this road Lenin and his aides think it possible to commit all crimes, such as the bloody fight in Petrograd, the devastation of Moscow, the annulment of free speech, the senseless arrests . . .
>
> Of course under the existing circumstances he does not believe in the possibility of a victory for the proletariat of Russia, but perhaps he hopes that a miracle will save the proletariat . . . One must understand that Lenin is not an all-powerful magician but a deliberate juggler, who has no feeling either for the lives or the honour of the proletariat.
>
> The working class must not allow adventurers and madmen to thrust upon the proletariat the responsibility for the disgraceful, senseless, and bloody crimes for which not Lenin, but the proletariat will have to account.

Lenin's response to this criticism was immediate and incisive. He declared the need for ruthlessness by the Government:

> As the State is only a transitional institution which we are obliged to use in the revolutionary struggle in order to crush our opponents forcibly, it is a pure absurdity to speak of a Free People's State. During the period when the proletariat still needs the State, it does not require it in the interests of freedom, but in the interests of crushing its antagonists.

61

In practice this declaration was to mean the suppression of Liberal, Menshevik and Socialist Revolutionary newspapers, and in December 1917 the outlawing of the Kadet Party. The freedom of opinion won by the Provisional Government was lost in the space of two months.

The Civil War and Terror which followed the Bolshevik coup were not accidents or unfortunate by-products of disorder, they were inevitable given the situation. A small minority had filled the power vacuum in the capital and immediately faced hostile groups and individuals who saw no reason to accept Bolshevik legitimacy, and were forced into either remaining silent or reacting violently themselves. Probably Lenin would have preferred to govern without Terror, but he was quite sanguine about applying it in what he considered to be an atmosphere of class conflict. 'How can one make revolution without executions?', he asked Kamenev soon after the coup. To Trotsky he remarked: 'Do you really think that we shall be victorious without using the most cruel terror?' Lenin had in the past expressed the opinion that the old Populist tactic of assassinating individual Government officials was unhelpful. But his views on the legitimacy of ruthless treatment of 'class enemies' en masse were very different. Advocates of moderation were brushed aside. Lenin instead authorised the feared Dzerzhinsky to implement a regime of Terror against enemies of the people.

CIVIL WAR AND FOREIGN INTERVENTION

Dzerzhinsky was instructed by Lenin to set up the Extraordinary Commission for Combating Counter-Revolution and Speculation (CHEKA) in December 1917. The CHEKA arrested suspected political opponents, saboteurs and other 'counter-revolutionaries', and meted out summary justice. Lenin took full responsibility for the CHEKA's actions. Terror met Terror. There were saints and angels on neither side.

Soon Terror merged into Civil War. Members of non-Bolshevik Parties, workers protesting against shortages, dispossessed landowners, disgruntled Army officers – these and many others took up arms against the new regime. Soon these 'Whites' were funded by foreign governments or joined by foreign armies sent in the first instance to force Russia back into the war with Germany, then eventually to overthrow a Government which was feared and detested by the outside world.

At about the time the Civil War began, Lenin left his headquarters in the Smolny and travelled secretly to Moscow. Moscow was to be the new capital of Russia, since geographically it was more secure than Petrograd. On 11 March Lenin took up residence in the Hotel National, before moving into a small flat in the Kremlin. Here, from his three rooms, plus kitchen and bathroom, and guarded by a unit of crack troops, he directed operations as his Government fought for its life.

The Civil War and War of Foreign Intervention lasted from 1918 to 1921. The result, a victory for the Reds, was determined by a number of factors: among them Trotsky's brilliant leadership of the new Red Army; mistakes, lack of co-ordination and half-heartedness on the part of many of its enemies and the reluctance of many Russians to fight against the regime if it meant a return to tsarism or something similar. But what was Lenin's role?

One aspect of Lenin's role was to continue issuing draconian orders. More representatives of left-wing political groups like the SRs were arrested, implicated in plots against the Government. The Tsar and his family were shot in order to prevent them falling into enemy hands. Although he may not have ordered it himself Lenin did not regret their execution. In August 1918 Lenin ordered ruthless measures against rich peasants who were resisting the new regime, in particular its requisitioning of food:

> Ruthless war must be waged on the kulaks! Death to them! Hatred and contempt for the parties which support them – the Right Socialist Revolutionaries, the Mensheviks, and now the Left Socialist Revolutionaries! The workers must crush the kulak revolts with an iron hand, for the kulaks have formed an alliance with the foreign capitalists against the toilers of their own country.
>
> (*Civil War in the Villages*, August 1918)

On 30 August 1918 Lenin himself was the victim of terrorism. Leaving a meeting hall in Moscow he was shot at close range by Fanya Kaplan, a Socialist Revolutionary. She was reportedly executed, although a recent theory suggests that the affair may have been fabricated in order to provide the Reds with an excuse for the Red Terror, and that Kaplan was seen alive many years later. The official version remains that Lenin was hit in the neck and collarbone, but without sustaining serious injury. On the same day, Uritsky, Head of the Petrograd CHEKA, was assassinated. The two acts of terrorism were the signal for a new wave of arrests and executions by the CHEKA, often carried out on very slender evidence. Lenin continued to justify the violence:

> The CHEKA is putting into effect the dictatorship of the proletariat, and in this sense it is of inestimable value. Outside of force and violence, there is no way to suppress the exploiters of the masses. This is the business of the CHEKA and in this lies its service to the proletariat.

LENIN IN THE KREMLIN

Although Lenin was often absorbed in the activities of the CHEKA, he remained busy with the more orthodox business of Government and Party matters. The Politburo was set up in March 1919, consisting of Lenin, Trotsky, Stalin, Bukharin and Kamenev. Two other members were added in 1920. Theoretically the Politburo was responsible to the Central Committee. Power was very much in the hands of the Party, which was named the Communist Party in March 1918.

Lenin was the most powerful man in Russia, but like his successor, Stalin, his existence was relatively frugal. He shared the small Kremlin flat with Krupskaya, his sister Maria, and a maid. Unlike Stalin, Lenin did not cut himself off completely from contact with ordinary people. He travelled the city and its environs informally to talk to Muscovites. At weekends he often travelled into the countryside with Maria and their brother Dimitri. They would walk and hunt, play with village children, or talk to peasants. Lenin tried to remain a 'man of the people' despite his own bourgeois origins.

Lenin's day was regularly ordered. Work began at 11am, with a reading of papers and a series of meetings and conferences, each allotted a precise time. Dinner lasted from 5.00pm to 7.00pm, then Lenin was back at work. SOVNARKOM meetings might last until the early hours of the morning. Even after these had finished, Lenin might work alone until dawn. It was a hard regime, and not surprisingly Lenin expected others to adhere to a strict schedule. It became too much for Krupskaya, who became ill with overwork. Lenin, however, was more upset by Inessa Armand's death from cholera in 1920. It was believed by many that Lenin's own illness was brought on by grief at her death.

Lenin was uninterested in the trappings of power and had no time for personal flattery. He sometimes displayed irritation at the unMarxist emphasis on the individual to which he was subjected in the media even before his death, although he did little to try to halt it. In 1921 Lenin completed a Party questionnaire, with characteristically simple replies. He gave his age as 51 and described himself as being in good health. His wife and sister were his dependants. He listed English and German as languages in which he was competent, whereas his French and Italian were weak. In this Lenin was being modest. He listed the Volga region, his birthplace, as the part of Russia he knew best. He gave his basic occupation as writer, and declared that he belonged to the Union of Journalists. He had had no special training. Other than a simple listing of his Party functions, there was no particular indication of Lenin's stature.

Lenin combined a personal modesty with an intellectual arrogance that expressed itself in an unshakeable conviction that he was always right, at least in political matters. He was certainly a figure who could not be easily ignored. Gorky's biography of Lenin, published in 1924, painted a vivid picture of a man 'firmly believing in his calling, one who is deeply and fully conscious of his bond with the world outside and has thoroughly understood his role in the chaos of the world, the role of an enemy of chaos'. He went on:

> He enjoyed fun, and when he laughed, his whole body shook, really bursting with laughter, sometimes until tears came into his eyes. There was an endless scale of shade and meaning in his inarticulate 'Hm' – ranging from bitter sarcasm to cautious doubt, and there was often in it the keen humour given only to one who sees far ahead and knows well the satanic absurdities of life.

This was a very different Gorky from the hostile commentator of 1917. He had fallen under Lenin's spell, describing him in the following words:

> Squat and solid, with a skull like Socrates and the all-seeing eyes of a great deceiver, he often liked to assume a strange and somewhat ludicrous posture; throw his head backwards, then

incline it to the shoulder, put his hands under his armpits, behind the vest. There was in this posture something delightfully comical, something triumphantly cocky. At such moments his whole being radiated happiness.

His movements were lithe and supple and his sparing but forceful gestures harmonised well with his words, also sparing but abounding in significance. From his face of Mongolian cast gleamed and flashed the eyes of a tireless hunter of falsehood and of the woes of life-eyes that squinted, blinked, sparkled sardonically, or glowered with rage. The glare of those eyes rendered his words more burning and more poignantly clear.

Lenin was not an easy man to work with, although he usually prevented his own strong feelings about individuals from interfering in policy decisions. Thus he could utter very strong comments against colleagues like Bukharin or Trotsky, but happily continue working with them. Lenin possessed a vituperative tongue, but he did not retain the lifelong vindictiveness of a Stalin. What struck Lenin's contemporaries most was his natural sense of authority. The British agent Bruce Lockhart penned a portrait of Lenin, declaring him head and shoulders above Trotsky. He described Lenin as possessing 'tremendous will-power', 'relentless determination' and 'lack of emotion'. In contrast to Gorky, Lockhart found Lenin 'impersonal and almost inhuman'. So much so that 'The only appeal that one could make to him was to his sense of humour, which if sardonic, was highly developed'. If a wordy debate was going on in a cabinet meeting, Lenin would be working quietly, then he 'would look up from his work, give his decision in one sentence, and all would be peace'. (*Memoirs of a British Agent*, 1974).

A fellow-revolutionary, Victor Serge, added more details in 1920 about Lenin's appearance and qualities as a speaker:

Practically bald, his cranium high and bulging, his forehead strong, he had commonplace features: an amazingly fresh and pink face, a little reddish beard, slightly jutting cheek-bones, eyes horizontal but apparently slanted because of the laughter lines, a grey-green gaze at people, and a surpassing air of geniality and cheerful malice . . .

He was not a great orator not a first-rate lecturer. He employed no rhetoric and sought no demagogical effects. His vocabulary was that of a newspaper article, and his technique included diverse forms of repetition all with the aim of driving ideas in thoroughly, as one drives in a nail. He was never boring, on account of his mimic's liveliness and the reasoned conviction which drove him. His customary gestures consisted of raising his hand to underline the importance of what he said, and then bending towards the audience, smiling and earnest, his palms spread out in an act of demonstration: 'It is obvious, isn't it?' Here was a man of basic simplicity, talking to you honestly with the sole purpose of convincing you, appealing exclusively to your judgement, to facts and sheer necessity. 'Facts have hard heads', he was fond of saying . . .

(*V. Serge, Memoirs of a Revolutionary* 1963)

THE COMINTERN

Lenin took a direct interest in the Communist International or Comintern, set up in 1919 during the Civil War. This was far from being a distraction for Lenin. After the Revolution he was convinced that conditions were ripe for world proletarian revolution, particularly as central and eastern Europe was in chaos. Regimes were rising and falling, old nation states and empires were giving way before the forces of nationalism. Lenin hoped for a revolution in Germany, but was disappointed by the Social Democratic Government which emerged at the end of the war. The German Communists failed in an attempt to seize power in 1919. Lenin signed an agreement with the Hungarian Communist leader Bela Kun, but the latter's regime was short-lived. Later, Lenin pinned his hopes on the Comintern.

Although Zinoviev was president of the Comintern, Lenin exercised close supervision, convinced as he was that the survival of his regime and Communism itself depended on success in exporting revolution outside Russia. And yet he had displayed little interest in the politics of other states, showing far more concern about class differences than shades of political opinion. Diplomacy held no interest for Lenin. In fact it could get in the way of international revolution. Like many other revolutionaries, during the First World War he confused war-weariness in the belligerent countries with revolutionary feeling. Those with more realistic perceptions urged Lenin to come up with a foreign policy, should he ever come to power. Lenin's reply was to suggest a revolutionary war should European states not experience internal revolutions inspired from within.

Within two years of assuming power, it began to dawn upon Lenin that his hopes of world or European revolution were premature. In 1920 he ordered the Red Army to march into Poland following the Polish withdrawal from the Ukraine. The Red Army was halted before it reached Warsaw, peace had to be made, and the threat of Russia exporting revolution across Europe receded.

Lenin now concentrated on the strategy of secretly organising and subsidising Communist parties in other countries. A favourite tactic was to use legitimate political activity as a cover for subversion, somewhat ironic coming from a man who, during the First World War, had roundly condemned foreign Governments for signing secret treaties. In 1920 Lenin wrote *Left-Wing Communism, An Infantile Disorder*. This book urged foreign Communists to demonstrate their leadership to the workers by participating in trade unions and parliaments. The same Lenin wrote *Twenty One Points*, which outlined the rules and tactics to be adopted by other Communist Parties. This was the beginning of the network by which the Comintern exercised control over foreign Communist Parties modelled on the Soviet version. Lenin personally wrote the instructions on how the Comintern should operate in each country. He bitterly attacked revisionists such as those moderates in the British Labour Party who sought to better working conditions by gaining concessions from capitalist regimes, just as he had attacked similar 'ideological deviants' before the war. Once again, the ends justified the means:

> The Communists must be prepared to make every sacrifice, and, if necessary, even resort to all sorts of cunning, schemes, and stratagems to employ illegal methods, to evade and conceal the truth, in order to penetrate into the trade unions, to remain in them, and conduct the Communist work in them at all costs.

> The task, wrote Lenin to his colleagues, was to discredit the 'incorrigible leaders of opportunism and of social chauvinism'.

In this sense, Trotsky, with his emphasis upon 'world revolution' rather than 'Socialism in one country', was the heir of Lenin, rather than Stalin, who was to focus very much upon building Socialism inside the USSR. And yet, for all the considerable time and energy which Lenin devoted to the rules and activities of the Comintern, it was already evident during his lifetime that few short-term gains were to be expected. He came to accept that Socialism could not be victorious in all European countries simultaneously, and that 'all nations will not reach Socialism in the same way'. It would be going too far to say that Lenin lost his revolutionary idealism, but towards the end of his life his Government was prepared to sign deals with the German and British Governments, even if an underlying distrust and willingness to take advantage of the others' difficulties always persisted.

WAR COMMUNISM
—

Another crucial concern of Lenin during the Civil War was the economy. The Russian economy was already in a critical state at the time of the Revolution – massive inflation and shortages of basic commodities were just two of the problems – but the crisis worsened as World War was replaced by Civil War and everyday economic life was continuously disrupted.

Lenin had given thought to Russia's economic situation in the months leading up to the October Revolution. Some of his interpretations were simplistic, such as his assertion that many of the problems could be attributed to the greed of industrialists and businessmen. From this argument he concluded that a Socialist Government would face few problems, because goodwill would be the order of the day, and involving the masses in decision-making would release new creative energies. Lenin was either being naive or deliberately glossing over anticipated problems for political reasons, although he was not utopian enough to suggest that workers could simply take over all management functions after a revolution, rather that existing managements should be supervised by workers or their representatives. In May 1917 he proposed nationalisation of banks and large conglomerates, but he did not advocate the nationalisation of medium-sized and small-sized businesses. His views on the land issue were more ambivalent: Lenin realised that poorer peasants did not have the capital or equipment to benefit from owning their own land, yet he also realised that nationalisation of the land would be badly received by many peasants. In August 1917 Lenin announced that the Bolsheviks did not support the nationalisation of land.

Lenin was moderate in his economic views in comparison with some colleagues like Bukharin. But none of the Bolsheviks quite anticipated the difficulties which they faced. After moving to Moscow in 1918, Lenin confidently asserted that Socialism would be achieved within six months. However, there was no blueprint from which to work, there was no common understanding of what Socialism entailed, nor indeed was there a compliant population. Lenin had already discovered this: within weeks of the Revolution he was complaining first that the soviets were holding too many meetings rather than getting things done, then that many workers were not co-operating with the new regime, and that, indeed, some were striking.

The period between 1918 and 1921 came to be known as the period of War Communism, but the directives which instituted changes in economic practice were not carefully thought out and introduced as part of a coherent plan. Rather they were brought in piecemeal in response to the critical circumstances which prevailed in Russia. This is not to say that there was not a strong ideological element to War Communism, simply that considerations of ideology were tinged with a strong dose of pragmatism. For example, measures to limit private trade, to fix prices, and in places to do away with money completely in favour of barter and free provision of basic services, arose from the breakdown of the existing balance between supply and demand, not because the Government planned it. The peasants wanted manufactured goods, but were unwilling to sell their grain because money was worthless. Measures like the forced requisitioning of the peasants' grain by the CHEKA were the response of a regime desperate to feed the towns, although it was also easy enough to give such measures an ideological gloss. Lenin certainly either initiated or supported the draconian measures which were enforced, without compunction.

A law on nationalisation was implemented in June 1918. Large enterprises were taken over by the State. Many smaller enterprises followed in December. Problems of production persisted. Many of the best personnel were serving and dying in the Red Army. Lenin used the old administrators and civil servants, with few qualms, although he was to admit later that Russia was turning into a 'workers' State with bureaucratic distortions'. His own remedy, that of having management constantly under scrutiny by the workforce, was frankly unworkable. Party officials were more adept as watchdogs. The notion of grass-roots supervision gave way before the trend of the Party acting as an increasingly authoritarian and monopolistic force.

A CULTURAL REVOLUTION?

Lenin was genuinely concerned, as he put it, to eliminate barbarism and to raise the 'cultural level' of the Russian people. To this end a series of laws was issued after the Revolution. Some were utopian: for example, a law of December 1919 which decreed that the illiterate, who comprised over half the country's population, should attend school. The logistics of this were simply impossible in the short term. But the intent was there, even if Lenin was revising his timetable. In December 1919 he declared: 'We know that we cannot establish a socialist system now: God grant that it may be established in our children's time, or perhaps in our grandchildren's time.'

Lenin in 1920

Lenin was to focus more attention on education as the Civil War drew to a close. He decided that a well-educated population was essential if progress were to be made towards Communism in a backward society. It was no use if only a few specialists or engineers understood the principles of modernisation. The whole population must learn and understand. Thus Lenin believed in a broad offensive on the educational front rather than a programme of sheer political indoctrination. All schoolchildren should learn not just the principles of Socialism but also the principles of subjects like agronomy and electrification. The latter subject in particular had a fascination for Lenin.

Lenin optimistically assumed that the cultural advancement of the people would blossom alongside economic development. He had great faith in technology, but he also emphasised the importance of intellectuals: these, with the benefits of their education, would bring culture to the masses. Urban intellectuals would spread enlightenment in the countryside – Lenin never doubted that progress equalled city life. Nevertheless, although he was advocating a 'cultural revolution', Lenin was an orthodox Marxist to the extent that he believed culture changed slowly, resulting from social and economic development. Cultural progress was impossible without a 'certain material base.'

Lenin was very appreciative of the cultural accomplishments of western civilisation. Unlike Stalin, he was not suspicious of them. Lenin appreciated the need for 'specialisation' and was prepared to welcome 'bourgeois specialists' into Russia. Whatever their political views, they had useful skills to teach to Communists. The native population would be slow to develop a 'proletarian culture'. The Russians must build upon the best of the past. Lenin opposed the destruction of old Russian monuments. Drastic measures would achieve nothing in the field of culture, since culture evolved organically.

Lenin himself liked the old Russian classics, and thought there was nothing reprehensible in the working class liking them also. He did not particularly appreciate some of the revolutionary art forms emerging, such as the 'proletarian' poetry of Mayakovsky. He was more at home with the press. With its obvious political potential, there was a means of communication which Lenin understood perfectly.

Back in 1901 Lenin had argued for the organisation of a national newspaper as a priority for the revolutionary movement. Such a development would assist in the growth of a Party organisation. In other

Тов. Ленин ОЧИЩАЕТ

землю от нечисти.

A 1920 Communist cartoon: 'Comrade Lenin cleans the world of filth'

words, propaganda and organisation were two sides of the same coin. The skill of the Bolsheviks as propagandists had certainly assisted the growth of their Party after February 1917, when censorship had disappeared. At the time of the Revolution, Lenin had not devoted much thought to the issue of censorship. The assumption that the Revolution would be a mass movement did not seem to necessitate censorship. However, Lenin soon came round to a perception of its desirability. He argued that bourgeois ideology was older and more developed than a proletarian one, and therefore possessed advantages which had to be countered. After the October Revolution SOVNARKOM published a decree permitting it to close newspapers which advocated resistance to the Government. The decree was supposed to be temporary.

The Bolsheviks did not proceed to the immediate suppression of all newspapers which did not follow their line. But Liberal and many Socialist newspapers were closed down by mid 1918. Lenin had his own opinions on what Bolshevik newspapers should contain: articles should be simple, concise, and deal with real situations if they were to have popular appeal. Soviet newspapers should not devote too much space to politics:

> Less political noise. Less *intelligent*-like discussions. Closer to life. More attention to how the masses of workers and peasants *in fact* build something new in their everyday work. More *documentation* of just how *communist* this new era is.
>
> ('About the Character of our Newspapers' in *Pravda*,
> September 1918.)

Lenin wanted the publication of details about which factories were working well, and which ones were not, and who were 'class enemies'. It was certainly not Lenin's intention to have theoretical discussions in the press about major political, social or economic issues, since those decisions had already been taken.

MOUNTING PROBLEMS

The first three years in power were extraordinarily difficult for the Communists, grappling with internal and external enemies, and trying to cope with a devastated economy. There were no easy solutions, just plenty of blood, sweat and tears. What began as utopianism quickly degenerated for many people into a grim struggle for survival. There were ardent Communists whose motto was 'never compromise', and who would have continued with 'necessary' measures, however unpopular they were with the ordinary people. Lenin, the chief political authority in the country, could not subordinate everything to some theoretical vision of a Socialist society. He recognised the truth. Compromise, or even retreat, was necessary if the regime were to survive. Compromise particularly on the economic front. Evidence of rising discontent was abundant. A decision to change economic strategy was made even before the spark of the Kronstadt Rebellion of 1921. Yet Lenin was determined enough to resist political compromise at the same time as loosening the reins of economic control. He was certainly not prepared to relax the monopoly of power which his regime enjoyed. The very future of Socialism was still too fraught with danger for that risk to be taken. It was not yet time for the State to 'wither away'.

timeline	1917 October	October Revolution
	November	Elections to Constituent Assembly
		CHEKA created
	December	Armistice with Germany
	1918 January	Constituent Assembly dissolved
	March	Treaty of Brest-Litovsk with Germany
		Bolsheviks became the Communist Party
		The Government moved to Moscow
	July	Execution of royal family
	August	Lenin shot
	1919 March	Comintern set up in Moscow
	1920 July	Tambov Revolt
	1921 March	Kronstadt Rebellion

Points to consider

1) Why did Lenin accept the Treaty of Brest-Litovsk in 1918?
2) Explain Lenin's policy towards the Constituent Assembly.
3) How important was Lenin's role in the Government and Communist Party between 1918 and 1920?
4) To what extent was Lenin responsible for the Red Terror?
5) What was the role of the Comintern?
6) Examine critically Lenin's views on the economy and Socialism during the period of War Communism.
7) Did Lenin initiate a cultural revolution after the October Revolution?
8) How successful was Lenin as Russia's leader during the period 1918-20?

NATIONAL RECOVERY, PERSONAL DECLINE

THE KRONSTADT REBELLION

The Kronstadt Rebellion broke out on 1 March 1921. It was only one in a series of expressions of violent discontent which swept Russia three years after the Revolution. Although the White armies had been defeated and Allied Governments were steadily losing interest in direct intervention, the Communist Government was still threatened. The privations of War Communism and a disenchantment with the increasingly dictatorial and arbitrary nature of Lenin's regime fuelled opposition within Russia. Although both workers and peasants were accustomed to economic hardship and harsh rule, there was no particular reason for them to love the Communist Party, whose promise of better things increasingly rang hollow. Mutinies in the Red Army, strikes and peasant risings, particularly in the Tambov region, were serious enough, but a revolt by the sailors of Kronstadt was of particular strategic and psychological significance. The sailors had been amongst the keenest supporters of the Bolsheviks in 1917 and helped them to power in Petrograd. Now they were protesting against the decline in power of the local soviets and the suppression of dissenting opinion, and they were calling for radical political changes.

Lenin was quick to brand the Rebellion as counter-revolutionary, inspired by the agents of foreign governments and Menshevik and Socialist Revolutionary dissenters. He dismissed it as 'a very petty incident' in an interview on 26 March, but on the following day gave a more honest assessment, describing the Rebellion as 'a flash of lightning which threw more of a glare upon reality than anything else.' That reality was, said Lenin, that

> There are only two kinds of government possible in Russia – a government by the soviets or a government headed by a tsar. Some fools or traitors in Kronstadt talked of a constituent assembly, but does any man in his senses believe for a moment that a constituent assembly at this critical abnormal stage would be anything but a bear garden?
>
> (Interview with *New York Herald Tribune*, 15 March 1921)

Lenin was being disingenuous, because Russia was ruled by the Communist Party, not the soviets. But his message was clear. Lenin told a meeting of transport workers on 27 March that 'more proletarian solidarity and discipline' were required to rectify the situation.

Lenin's interpretation of 'discipline' was unambiguous: the Rebellion was ruthlessly crushed by Trotsky and Tukhachevsky. Thousands of rebels were shot during the recapture of Kronstadt, or were executed in cold blood afterwards.

It was entirely in character for Lenin to have no compunction about shedding blood to save the regime; then formulating a theoretical argument to demonstrate why his response was necessary and justified; and finally to adopt the pragmatic approach of considering what had gone seriously wrong, and what changes in policy should be made. This was typical of Lenin's approach, whatever objections might be voiced by some of the 'purists' in the Party, who would have always put ideological considerations before practical ones.

THE NEW ECONOMIC POLICY

In fact, changes in policy were already under consideration. The Kronstadt Rebellion simply concentrated minds more narrowly on the future path of the Government. Economic problems were the prime concern. The key to economic change, with the intention of pacifying workers and peasants and stimulating production and trade, was the abandoning of War Communism and its replacement by the New Economic Policy.

Lenin accepted that the peasants in particular had legitimate complaints. He conceded in March 1921 that 'the Peasantry had to save the State by accepting the surplus-grain appropriations without remuneration, but it can no longer stand the strain.' Lenin told the Tenth Congress of the Party that:

> In essence the small farmer can be satisfied with two things. First of all, there must be a certain amount of freedom of turnover, of freedom for the small private proprietor; and secondly, commodities and products must be provided.

Under NEP peasants were freed from the threat of requisitioning and were allowed to engage in private enterprise, selling surplus food in return for the goods which they wanted, once they had paid their taxes. Other important changes were made. Private enterprise was legalised. Small producers could trade freely. Concessions were made to foreign investors. However, in addition to land, major industries and the transport system, what Lenin called 'the commanding heights of the economy', remained nationalised, as did foreign trade. This was the mixed economy to which Lenin gave the name 'state capitalism'.

NEP was to have a profound impact upon the Soviet economy. It certainly stimulated private enterprise and led to increased output and trade, although the stability provided by the final ending of seven years of World and Civil War was another factor in helping the Soviet economy to breathe again. This was the economic system which was to operate beyond Lenin's death, until 1928, when collectivisation of agriculture and the introduction of the Five-Year Plans were to initiate an even more drastic revolution in the economic system.

NEP was never a comfortable fact of life for the Communist Party. To those enthusiastic Party members who had been through the fires of Revolution and Civil War, and who believed that ruthless measures were necessary in order to build a Socialist heaven upon earth, NEP was at best an unsatisfactory compromise between Socialism and capitalism, at worst an outright betrayal of Marxism. Under NEP, the class of wealthy peasants, the kulaks, prospered in the free market conditions, whilst 'Nepmen' could make a living by speculation rather than honest productive labour. To many Communists these unwelcome developments were simply the symptom of a deeper malaise.

Lenin and NEP

Lenin's own position on NEP was somewhat ambivalent. The Marxist historian Christopher Hill claimed that Lenin 'never attempted to disguise the fact that it (NEP) was a large-scale retreat, another breathing-space, a Brest-Litovsk on the economic front.' (*Lenin and the Russian Revolution*, 1947.) In reality, Lenin's position was not so clear-cut. Certainly his initial response in 1921 was that NEP was a 'strategic retreat', an unpleasant necessity. In October 1921 he told an audience of Moscow Communists that they had suffered a defeat on the economic front more serious than anything which had taken place during the Civil War. He told them: 'Let us retreat and construct everything in a new and solid manner; otherwise we shall be beaten.'

However, it was characteristic of Lenin that, although he was very conscious of the practical necessity of the changes being made, that alone was not a sufficient rationale, and he sought ways of justifying NEP in terms of Marxist ideology. Lenin argued that economically, Russia was too backward a State to permit a rapid transition to Socialism. This in itself represented a change from some earlier positions. Lenin regarded the mentality of the peasants in particular as being too 'petty-bourgeois' for them to become Socialists overnight. They must be influenced 'morally'. This emphasis on the gradualness of change was to be taken up in one of Lenin's last works, *On Co-operation*, dictated in January 1923. In this article Lenin reversed his old sneers against gradual reformers. Now that the Party was in control, it was precisely the patient, educational work which mattered, rather than dramatic flourishes:

> Heroism displayed in prolonged and stubborn organisational work on a national scale is immeasurably more difficult than, but at the same time immeasurably superior to, heroism displayed in an insurrection.

Lenin concluded that there had to be a transition period between the fledgling capitalist State which Russia was in 1921, and the Socialist State which it would eventually become. That transition period would last several years, and would be characterised by 'State capitalism'. Although private enterprise was now permitted, the interests of the workers would be guarded by the State. Eventually the people's outlook would mature and fully-fledged Socialism would be possible. In the meantime, even the experience of the enemy should be utilised: 'No price for tuition will be too high if only we learn intelligently.'

Having given a theoretical justification for NEP, Lenin went on to enthuse about its role in leading Russia to Socialism:

> No matter how difficult the problem may be, no matter what the obstacles that must be overcome or how many difficulties it may involve, we shall achieve it, not tomorrow, it is true, but surely in the course of the next few years, in such a way that the Russia of the NEP will be transformed into Socialist Russia.

And yet soon after writing this, Lenin declared:

> We have not even completed the foundation for a Socialist economic order.

In other words, Lenin veered between optimism and pessimism, as he was to on several issues towards the end of his life. But on this particular issue he was quite certain that for the sake of foreign comrades in particular, NEP must be defended as facilitating the path to world revolution. At a Party Congress in March 1922 Lenin poured scorn on those Communists who did not accept what he regarded as the spirit of NEP:

> The capitalist is operating by your side. He is operating like a robber, he makes a profit, but he is skilful. But you – you are trying to do it in a new way: you do not make any profit; your Communist principles, your ideals are excellent, they are written out so beautifully that you deserve to be living saints in heaven – but can you do business?

Lenin's message was: Communism had to mean something real and material, particularly for the peasants, if it were to be successful. Hence Lenin's famous dictum that 'Communism equals Soviet power plus the electrification of the whole country.' This was the paradox of the leader personally uninterested in material benefits, but who preached the benefits of materialism for the masses.

After Lenin's death, debates about the economy were to take on a new significance, as ideological arguments about economic systems became part of the struggle for power amongst Lenin's associates. All the leading figures in the Party, whatever their views on NEP, were agreed that eventually Russia must industrialise, as the first pre-requisite for Socialism. The real argument concerned the correct path to this goal. The Left, represented by Trotsky, argued for taxation of the peasants to provide the resources to pay for industrialisation. The Right, represented by Bukharin, argued that peasant enterprise should be encouraged, on the grounds that prosperous peasants would buy goods, stimulate the industrial market, and so boost the economy. Lenin died before the arguments were really under way, so we cannot be sure of the stance he would have taken over the continuation of NEP had he lived much longer. The decision to requisition grain from the peasants in the late 1920s, a reversion to War Communism, and then the decision to collectivise, were taken after the peasants, dissatisfied with low prices for their produce, showed a renewed reluctance to supply the towns with food. There is no reason to suppose from Lenin's earlier career that he would not have authorised similar actions himself had the situation demanded drastic measures. Whether Lenin would have instituted such a ruthless programme of liquidating kulaks, forcibly collectivising, and implementing such a vast scheme of industrial planning, it is difficult to say. The relationship of Leninism to the methods of Stalinism is an issue which will be addressed later.

THE 1921 CONGRESS

It would be misleading to label 1921 the year of retreat for Lenin. Economic retreat there was, perhaps. But at the same time that NEP was introduced, Lenin made political moves designed to reinforce the authority of the Party and cohesion within it. It was almost as if Lenin took a calculated decision that if economic concessions were to be made, then the leadership of the Party must have complete confidence that its dictates would be obeyed. This equation may not have been the sole reason for decisions taken at the 1921 Congress to clamp down on political dissent. There had already been worrying signs for the leadership. Almost inevitably after 1917, once the Bolsheviks had become the Party of power, however precariously, a number of opportunists or hangers-on joined them. Concern about the quality of Party membership resulted in moves in 1921 to investigate every Party member, in order to check credentials. Every Party member, including Lenin, completed a questionnaire about his or her background.

There was also the perceived problem of opposition to the leadership from some committed elements within the Party. A group called the Workers' Opposition contained Communists who were critical of centralising tendencies within the Party apparatus, tendencies which reduced the role and status of trade unions and prevented genuine 'workers' democracy'. Although Lenin himself lived unostentatiously, there were complaints about the growth of privilege amongst Party members.

Lenin ordered the disbanding of the Workers' Opposition, which he referred to as a 'syndicalist absurdity', on the grounds that if the workers, of whom only a minority were Party members, were given too much say in the running of industry, then 'What need is there of the Party?' Presumably this was a rhetorical question. No questioning of the need for a Party could be tolerated, it was Lenin's very reason for existing. However, the issue went deeper. According to Lenin, 'There can be no question of independence on the part of separate groups.' He was unhappy at the amount of time taken up in the Party by arguments such as those about the status of trade unions. Arguments developed into factions, and factions could threaten the leadership.

Soviet Russia in 1921 was beset by internal problems and enemies, and faced a hostile world, ready to take advantage of any sign of disunity or weakness within Party ranks. Therefore, at the same time as economic controls were relaxed, political ones must be tightened. At the Tenth Party Congress of March 1921 a strict ban was to be imposed on 'factionalism' within the Party. Whilst Party members might legitimately discuss certain issues, there must be a unity of purpose and a ban on any separate platforms.

Lenin prepared the ground carefully. He got trusted colleagues to work on non-aligned delegates at the Congress, and won back support from some groups pledged to support opposing views. Lenin drafted the key resolutions:

'It is essential that all politically-conscious workers should clearly understand the danger and impermissibility of any factionalism whatsoever which inevitably will lead in fact to the weakening of harmonious work and to the intensified and repeated attempts by enemies who have attached themselves to the ruling party to deepen the division and utilise it for counterrevolution.

The example of recent events in Kronstadt was quoted by Lenin in support of his case. The remedy, went on Lenin, was propaganda in support of the correct line and a vigorous campaign within the Party against factional groups. It was necessary to purge 'non-proletarian and unreliable elements' and to fight against 'bureaucratism'. Expulsion from the Party awaited those who refused to heed the call for unity.

Lenin secured the election of a new Central Committee, although some members of the defeated opposition were included in order to appease dissenters. The Party rank and file was content with the changes. Lenin's Secretariat sent some members of the Workers' Opposition to carry out tasks in the provinces in order to keep them out of the way. In this respect Lenin was more moderate than his successor Stalin, who preferred to liquidate doubters within the Party rather than send them on long journeys.

The significance of Lenin's decisions at the Tenth Congress should not be underrated. It would be simplistic to accuse Lenin of imposing a Stalinist monopoly of ideology on his colleagues and the country. For all his often peremptory dismissal of opponents' arguments, and his tendency to spice his own arguments with abuse of those opponents, Lenin was not afraid to argue a case. He did not demand that people even *think* like himself. Perhaps it was for this reason that Lenin did not impose his own views on culture in the authoritarian way that Stalin was to. Lenin had his own opinions, but he knew that he could not transform a people's psychology overnight, even if the ultimate aim was the universal spread of a proletarian consciousness. Lenin at this stage was concerned chiefly with keeping a united Party at the helm and on course. Western liberal arguments about the virtues of free political debate meant nothing to him. However, the ban on factionalism was to become a potent weapon in the hands of those who succeeded Lenin, particularly Stalin. It became philosophically difficult for committed Communists to speak out against the prevailing Party line without being accused of encouraging factionalism and threatening the country's security. In this sense 1921 certainly was a step on the path to a totalitarian State, a step for which Lenin unwittingly bore a major responsibility.

DECLINING HEALTH

The trials of the spring of 1921 behind him, Lenin might have hoped to devote more time to the recovery of Russia and the implementation of his ideas. Unfortunately for Lenin, it was later that year that his health began to seriously deteriorate. Tiredness, giddiness, an inability to sleep, all convinced him that he was seriously ill, and in December he informed his Politburo colleagues that he would be unable to make his usual report to the next Party Congress. Instead he rested at his home in Gorki, although he continued to dictate policies.

Lenin did attend the Eleventh Party Congress, in March 1922 – his last one – but in the same month Russian and foreign doctors examined him. In April an operation was performed to remove one of the bullets left in his body after the assassination attempt of 1918. But it was to no avail. Lenin suffered his first stroke in May 1922. Gradual paralysis seriously affected his body. His mind was unaffected.

The Central Committee supervised Lenin's medical care. He was nursed principally by his sister, Maria, and Krupskaya. Lenin gradually fought his way back to health, and in the summer he was visited by colleagues at Gorki. Although forbidden to talk business, Lenin retained an interest in State affairs, particularly a much publicised trial of Socialist Revolutionary leaders held in Moscow between June and August.

Lenin recovered sufficiently to return to Moscow in October 1922. He was allowed by his doctors to work for five hours a day, with two days of rest a week. The old routine was revived in a truncated form: chairing meetings of the Politburo and SOVNARKOM, seeing visitors, reading reports, issuing orders, even attending a meeting of the Fourth Congress of the Comintern.

This routine lasted only until November, when the old symptoms of illness returned. Although Lenin still read copiously, he increasingly withdrew from the day-to-day business of government. He suffered a second serious stroke in December 1922. Lenin rested, then resumed reading and writing against his doctors' advice. In mid December he began to put his affairs in order and to dictate his last letters and

Lenin and Krupskaya at Gorki in 1922

commands. On 25 and 26 December he dictated, over four sessions, his famous *Testament*.

WORRIES ABOUT THE SUCCESSION

The struggle about who should succeed Lenin as leader had already begun, as soon as it was obvious that he was seriously ill. Trotsky, Zinoviev and Stalin were the chief contenders. Zinoviev, Kamenev and Stalin effectively ran the Party in Lenin's absence. Trotsky began to oppose them, although his position was not strong: he lacked a Party base, and following victory in the Civil War and the suppression of the Kronstadt Rebellion, his importance in terms of practical politics had declined. All members of the Politburo jockeyed for position to a greater or lesser extent, but Stalin did so the most effectively, through his role as General Secretary, which allowed him to promote his protegés in the Party machine and to prepare Party agendas.

Despite the ban on factions, internecine fighting was already well under way between Party leaders. Lenin now had to grapple with this situation in his *Testament*. Lenin considered the qualities of the protagonists:

> Comrade Stalin, having become General Secretary, has concentrated enormous power in his hands, and I am not sure that he always knows how to use that power with sufficient caution. On the other hand, Comrade Trotsky ... is distinguished not only by his exceptional ability – personally, he is, to be sure, the most able man in the present Central Committee – but also by his too far-reaching self-confidence and a disposition to be far too much attracted by the purely administrative side of affairs.

Little was said about other members of the Central Committee. Reference was made to the opposition of Kamenev and Zinoviev to Lenin's proposal for a coup in September 1917. Bukharin was praised for his great intellectual ability, but Lenin cast doubts on his Marxist credentials, possibly because he had disagreed with Lenin on several economic issues in the past. Piatakov, like Trotsky, was 'too given over to the administrative side of affairs to be relied upon in serious political questions'. Rather patronisingly, Lenin conceded that Bukharin and Piatakov, being younger and well-meaning, might yet 'find occasion to supplement their knowledge and correct their one-sidedness'.

Ten days later, on 4 January 1923, Lenin added a postscript, following Stalin's rudeness to Krupskaya in a telephone conversation. Lenin condemned Stalin's behaviour and proposed that the Party should replace Stalin as General Secretary. Comrades should look for a man 'more patient, more loyal, more polite, and more attentive to comrades, less capricious, etc'. Not all of these qualities were notable characteristics of Lenin himself, but he was clearly worried.

On 5 March 1923 Lenin was to send a letter to Stalin, complaining again about the treatment of his wife:

> I have no intention to forget so easily that which is being done against me, and I need not stress here that I consider as directed against me that which is being done against my wife. I ask you, therefore, that you weigh carefully whether you are

agreeable to retracting your words and apologising or whether you prefer the severance of relations between us.

The *Testament* was hardly a satisfactory legacy from Lenin to his Party and country. It offered no clear directive on how Lenin saw the future. He seemed to be suggesting that no one person had the qualities to replace him. Presumably he hoped for a collective leadership, combining the qualities of several men, although this was not spelt out. This was not simply arrogance on Lenin's part: his authority had not rested on any official position but upon his career and achievements to date. No one person *could* succeed Lenin by virtue of any official post alone. Exceptional personal qualities would be necessary. However, Lenin gave no indication that he felt any personal blame for the situation. He had appointed Stalin to the post of General Secretary. Although the post was not quite so important as it was to become later, Lenin appears not to have noticed the signs of Stalin's growing power until it was too late. Then he could offer no solution other than a pious hope that comrades would be able to remove Stalin. Lenin had not given enough thought to the structure of the Party's leadership, and in the last resort power and influence rested not upon consensus and responsibility to the membership, but on the ability of individuals to manipulate support and build their own power bases. It was little different from the days of power struggles in medieval Russia; and those who combined ruthlessness with cunning had a great advantage over those who were skilled only in the arts of political debate. It would have been difficult to introduce quickly into Russia a more open system of promotion by merit, which might have prepared the way for a less arbitrary path to the top, but there is no evidence that Lenin really tried an alternative. Of course he was seriously ill during the last two years of his life. But the danger signs had already been there, and the Bolsheviks had always been a conspiratorial Party before 1917, so their methods of doing things did not change radically after the Revolution. Lenin's *Testament* comes dangerously close to being a Testament of despair.

Lenin intended his *Testament* to be read to the Twelfth Congress of the Party. But Krupskaya kept it secret, hoping that her husband would recover his health. After Lenin's death, she gave the *Testament* to the Central Committee and demanded that it be read at the Thirteenth Congress, due to meet in May 1924. Stalin and his colleagues agreed to have the documents read to individual delegations, but it was not made public out of a desire to preserve unity in the Party. The *Testament* was published in the USSR in 1956.

FINAL THOUGHTS

Lenin remained busy until a few months before his death. His last article was titled 'Better Fewer, But Better'. It was dictated during January and February 1923 and published in *Pravda* on 4 March. It is an interesting document, because Lenin indulged in some soul-searching about the past and the future. He wrestled with problems of government and bureaucracy, whilst trying to defend the regime that had developed. He continued to defend the right to employ Terror under the New Economic Policy as the ultimate weapon of defence. He argued for a broad definition of 'counter-revolutionary activity': propaganda and agitation which would help the 'international bourgeoisie' should be capital offences. But in other areas Lenin preached moderation and caution. For example, 'In matters of culture, haste and sweeping measures are most harmful. Many of our young writers and Communists should get this well into their heads.' The Government should proceed slowly: 'Our State apparatus is so deplorable, not to say wretched.' Things must be put right gradually: 'We must show sound scepticism for too rapid progress, for boastfulness etc.' The rule to follow was 'Better fewer, but better.' It was necessary for the Party to learn, even by sending its people abroad to hostile countries like Britain in order to learn from experienced administrators. 'We just reduce our State apparatus to the utmost degree of economy.' But the working class must retain leadership over the economy.

Lenin was wrestling with important issues. He did not seem fully aware of the extent to which the abuse of power and dictatorship was made possible by the Soviet regime, or rather he naively assumed that a rational authoritarian regime was possible if operated by men of integrity. In his utopianism he did not solve the problem of reconciling discipline with efficiency. There must be the possibility of criticism if the Party were not to degenerate into a totally unresponsive bureaucracy, but how could criticism be prevented from developing into factionalism?

In these final thoughts Lenin was certainly considering major changes. He was even prepared to restructure the recently created

Union if it would solve the Nationalities problem. His plans to enlarge the Central Committee and reduce the powers of the Secretariat and Party Executive were likewise designed to defeat internal opposition to reforms from an entrenched and conservative bureaucracy. Unfortunately it was all too late.

DEATH

On 9 March 1923 Lenin suffered his third stroke, from which he never fully recovered. In May he was moved to Gorki. In the summer and autumn his health did improve to the extent that he was able to travel to Moscow. However, deterioration soon set in again. A severe attack on 21 January 1924 was soon followed by a haemorrhage of the brain, and death.

timeline		
1921	March	Tenth Party Congress. NEP announced
1922	April	Stalin appointed General Secretary
	May	Lenin suffered his first stroke
	December	Lenin suffered further strokes, and dictated *Testament*
1923	March	Lenin's third stroke
	July	Soviet Constitution published
1924	January	Death of Lenin

Points to consider

1) What was the significance of the Kronstadt Rebellion for Lenin?
2) How did Lenin justify the New Economic Policy?
3) What changes did Lenin make at the Tenth Party Congress, and why did he make them?
4) How convincingly did Lenin tackle the problems of government and the succession in the last two years of his life?

6

LEGACY

LENIN LAID TO REST?

Following a medical autopsy, Lenin's body was laid out in state in Moscow for the faithful to file past in homage. The sense of national grief was overwhelming. After the funeral the body was embalmed and placed in a granite mausoleum in Red Square. But Lenin could not be allowed to lie in peace. Only five days later, Lenin's eventual successor Stalin delivered a funeral oration to the Congress of Soviets. Stalin invoked Lenin's name in almost religious tones as a beacon to guide the Soviet Union into the future. It took only five days for the man to become a myth. Thereafter, Lenin was as important not just for what he had achieved, but as a slogan or icon by which legitimacy could be conferred on any idea or action promulgated by the Soviet Government, or indeed by any Marxist regime.

Ordinary people, thousands at a time, were to queue to see Lenin's body for decades to come. Some came out of curiosity, some out of a sense of patriotic duty, some out of reverence, some for ideological reasons, some from persuasion. For most Soviet citizens, and indeed for many foreigners, a visit to the Lenin mausoleum was a pilgrimage that had to be made at least once in a lifetime. And so far more people saw Lenin in death than had ever seen him alive. It became increasingly difficult to separate the man from what he stood for, or rather what others claimed he stood for.

A SOVIET HERO

Within the USSR Lenin remained at least as important after his death as before. His influence was all-pervasive, and he was beyond official criticism. When Gorbachev was arguing the case for *perestroika* or fundamental reconstruction in the 1980s, Lenin's name was invoked to lend respectability to the changes being implemented in the economy and society. Comparisons were made with Lenin's NEP. Only as the Communist Party began to lose its grip and the Soviet Union broke up were the first overt criticisms of Lenin tentatively attempted. Even when Lenin was no longer regarded as an icon, he was not classed with other Soviet leaders like Stalin and Brezhnev, who were roundly criticised for policies of repression and economic and social stagnation.

For more than two generations after his death, Lenin, as a symbol, was all things to all people – prophet, caring father of his people, and almost a religious leader rolled into one:

In Tadjik and Kazakh legend Lenin was as high as the hills, as the clouds; in Dungan folk-lore he was brighter than the sun and knew no night. The Oyruts say that he had a sunbeam in his right hand, a moonbeam, in his left; the ground trembled under him. For the Uzbeks Lenin was a giant who could shake the earth and move great rocks in his search for the fortune hidden in the hills; he could solve the most puzzling riddles. In Kirgiz story he had a magic ring, with the help of which he overthrew the power of the evil one and liberated the poor from wrong and injustice. He is reported to have arrived in Armenia on a white horse, to lead the people. In another legend Lenin was a Titan struggling against Asmodeus, the friend of the rich and privileged, the worst enemy of the poor. Asmodeus strove to kill Lenin, but the light from the hero's eyes put him to flight. Lenin then seated himself upon an eagle and flew to Dagestan where he stirred up war against the rich, and finally flew back to the cold regions to write books of truth for the people. For the northern Ostyaks Lenin was a great seal hunter who slew the rich fur-traders and gave the booty to the poor; similarly, the Nentsy think of Lenin as the most expert of all sailors, who overcame his enemies in combat, seized their dogs and reindeer, and divided them among the poor. Sholokhov's Cossacks visualised Lenin as a Don Cossack.

(C. Hill, *Lenin and the Russian Revolution*)

Generations of Soviet schoolchildren were brought up to believe in Lenin as both father-figure and god-substitute. A portrait of Lenin was on the back wall of every classroom. Lenin during his lifetime took a genuine delight in the company of children, and enthusiastically joined in their games, so it was a simple task for the Stalinist propaganda machine to build in these stories as part of a carefully-conceived indoctrination programme. By the time the children had grown to adulthood, those who went on to higher education were faced with library shelves groaning under the weight of Lenin's collected works, and attended lectures on Marxist-Leninist philosophy. All citizens could see daily the posters of Lenin and Leninist slogans on street corners and the sides of buildings. Big Brother was watching, a benign Big Brother except to those with nefarious designs on the Soviet State.

LENIN'S LEGACY

As the founder of the Soviet State and its institutions, Lenin's impact upon Russian history was clearly of fundamental importance. It is difficult to conceive of the October Revolution taking place without Lenin, despite the higher profile of Trotsky at the time. After the Revolution, in the few brief years before Lenin's death, there were important political, economic and social developments in Russia and its old Empire, not all directly attributable to Lenin, but most bearing his stamp in some way. Lenin took over an Empire which was breaking up, suffering from military defeat and in a state of economic and political crisis. Having weathered further years of internal strife, a gradual erosion of the political liberties apparently won in February 1917, and ruinous attempts to direct the economy from the centre, reversed in 1921, Lenin died in 1924. He left a Soviet State which was smaller territorially than the old Russian Empire, but which was asserting a far more thorough control over what remained than anything that the tsars had managed. The country on Lenin's death was economically poor, reviving, but still operating below 1913 levels of output. It was a country in which there was no political liberty in the western liberal sense,

1924 Poster: 'V.I. Ulyanov 1870-1924'

although this had always been the case in Russia apart from the brief period between the two Revolutions in 1917. Local democracy as represented by the soviets was eroded soon after the Bolshevik Revolution, a process hastened by the Civil War, which witnessed the steadily increasing power of the Party apparatus. Rival left-wing Parties had been eliminated by the time of Lenin's death. Policy discussions were still possible within the Communist Party, although any attempt to create a faction or a separate political platform was severly frowned upon, and likely to lead to disciplinary action.

Lenin also left Russia in a situation of cultural experimentation, if not ferment. As an intellectual, as well as a man of action, Lenin was widely-read and very conscious of the heritage of the past. Whilst accepting the desirability of a cultural awareness in keeping with the anticipated new Socialist world order, he had distinct reservations about forcing the pace of cultural changes from above. Lenin had been steeped in the old classics, although his own literary style was utilitarian, always designed to explain or inculcate a particular view. Lenin had been relatively tolerant of new forms of cultural experimentation, although he had disliked many of them personally. He had favoured educational changes which would give opportunities to all, but he had not wanted to throw out all expressions of old 'bourgeois culture', provided that learning was not confined to the élite. Culture belonged to the people, and the task of education was to raise the general level of literacy and understanding. The period to 1924 saw several experiments in education, and a flourishing of new art forms, including the cinema, a medium whose potential Lenin fully appreciated. There were some limitations to self-expression. The writer Yevgeny Zamyatin was a Bolshevik who soon after the Revolution began to chafe against the demands of Communist orthodoxy. In 1920 he wrote the novel *We*, one of the major inspirations for George Orwell's *1984*. The novel painted a totalitarian, dehumanised future, the result of Communist policies. The novel could not be published in Russia, and the author was attacked for his views, although he was not silenced until the more rigorous Stalinist climate at the end of the decade. The Leninist period was one of comparative tolerance. It was to be under Stalin that the State took control of all cultural expression.

THE LENINIST STATE

One of Lenin's early decrees after the Revolution concerned the separation of Church and State, which occurred in January 1918. As a Marxist, Lenin had no time for religion. Persecution of the Orthodox Church by means of depriving it of its property, arresting priests, and active discouragement of church services, began soon after the Revolution. Lenin's Russia was a secular State from the start, and it was to remain so for generations, although religious belief and practice survived waves of persecution and official discouragement.

To what extent was Lenin responsible for the bureaucratic, all-powerful State which is commonly associated with the Stalinist period?

The reality of Soviet Russia was that the State was never as totalitarian as it appeared on paper and was so described by its opponents. Moscow could never exercise complete control over distant provinces, and local centres of influence remained, where individuals in responsible Party positions could exercise local power, sometimes in an arbitrary fashion. But certainly many bureaucratic tendencies were evident in Lenin's Russia, and indeed had been a feature of past Russian regimes also; and certainly by Lenin's death Russia was a one-Party State, even if a revolutionary ethos persisted and a hierarchy of privilege had not yet quite ossified as it was to in later years, despite periodic purges.

Like most Marxists Lenin decried the two extremes of anarchism and excessive State power. In 1918 Lenin had estimated that the State would begin to wither away in about ten years. There was an implicit contradiction: The State had to be strong enough in order to destroy the last vestiges of bourgeois society, which would resist change, and yet also be capable of implementing its own destruction. This inner contradiction was never resolved. Those in power are usually reluctant to give it up. In Soviet Russia the organs of bureaucracy and State power simply became stronger. Lenin could offer no practical solutions, only epigrams like: 'So long as the State exists there is no freedom; when freedom exists there will be no State'. Lenin's successors never recognised that there was a dilemma: State power was always justified on the grounds that it was exercised in the interests of the people, not a ruling class.

In the post-Revolutionary chaos of Russia the administration simply broke down. It did not require destruction from above. But some form of administration was necessary, and Lenin had been forced to concede the need to employ thousands of administrators from the old regime. In 1921 he had declared: 'Can every worker know how to administer the State? Practical people know that this is a fairy tale.' Lenin spent his last years campaigning against excessive bureaucracy whilst urging more workers to join in. In a lecture which Lenin delivered at the Sverdlov University on 11 July 1919 he began by conceding to his audience that 'the question of the State is a most complex and difficult one'. It was an issue, he said, that could not be understood without detailed study. And yet by the end of the lecture Lenin himself had been reduced to little more than generalised utopian sentiments on the prospects for the future:

The machine which was called the State and before which people bowed in superstitious awe . . . this machine the proletariat casts aside and declares that it is a bourgeois lie. We have deprived the capitalists of this machine and have taken it for ourselves. With this machine, or bludgeon, we shall destroy all exploitation.

Lenin criticised bureaucrats who behaved like administrators with no long-term perspective, that is, apparatchiks who were so wrapped up in their work that it became the end in itself rather than a means to an end. For that reason he dismissed notions of forming new Government departments as 'pernicious twaddle'. Lenin feared that the bureaucracy was too separate from the Party and was threatening to make the Party its captive. He told the Eleventh Party Congress in 1922:

If we take Moscow with its 4,600 Communists in responsible positions, and if we take that huge bureaucratic machine, that gigantic heap, we must ask: who is directing whom? I doubt very much whether it can truthfully be said that the Communists are directing that heap. To tell the truth, they are not directing, they are being directed.

However, Lenin failed to take enough note of bureaucratisation *within* the Party. Lenin sometimes talked as if having 'the right people' at the helm would solve the problem. Trotsky took a broader view, seeing the problem of bureaucratisation as one created by the state of the economy, which could be put right by institutional measures and centralised planning. Lenin did come round to Trotsky's view late in life, particularly when arguments with Stalin over Nationalities issues seemed to suggest the dangers of bureaucratisation within the Party, with decisions being taken and implemented by Party members without due consideration of all the political implications.

The reality was that the organs of State power acquired their own ethos and privileges, and became as divorced from the life and concerns of ordinary citizens as they had ever been in tsarist days, even if bureaucrats now came from a wider social background. Lenin bequeathed this bureaucratic State to his successors. It is not what he wanted, but it is difficult to see how it could have been different given the

1970 Poster: 'Lenin lived, Lenin is living, Lenin will live!'

circumstances in which the Bolsheviks first came to power and then tried to cling on to it.

LENIN AND THE NATIONALITIES ISSUE

The Fifth Congress of Soviets was held in March 1918, and authorised the first Soviet Constitution, the Russian Soviet Federated Socialist Republic. The USSR was created in December 1922, but its Constitution was ratified only in January 1924, soon after Lenin's death. Negotiations were complicated mainly by the Nationalities issue, an issue which interested Lenin and was to be of significance for the entire future history of the Soviet Union until its break-up.

The old Russian Empire was a multi-national State, encompassing different peoples from the European borders in the West to the Pacific in the East. The subject nationalities had shown signs of unrest before, and continued to be a cause of concern to the Provisional Government after the February Revolution. Lenin addressed the problem at the Seventh Bolshevik Party Conference in April 1917. He declared that all the nations in the old Empire had the right of secession, although he expected that such a policy would win the trust of the non-Russians who would thereby wish to remain in a multi-national Socialist State which cared for the rights of all working people, whatever their nationality.

Thereafter Lenin was too pre-occupied with other issues to give much more attention to the Nationalities issue, other than a few short articles. However, after coming to power the problem had to be addressed. Immediately after the Revolution Lenin issued a decree conceding the right of self-determination to 'all the nations inhabiting Russia'. He recognised that Finland, Poland and the Ukraine were special cases that would wish to secede. However, he expected that the other nationalities would opt for a union with his new Russia. He appears to have been surprised by the strength of national feeling which emerged, because without giving a detailed explanation for his change in policy, he quickly came round to the view that a federal State was a possibility. The national groups would not accept a total union which would probably imply Russification, a subordination of their own interests and character to Russian interests.

Lenin created the People's Commissariat of Nationality Affairs to manage relationships with the nationalities. It was under Stalin. His task was to mediate in disputes between national groups. In practice, other than Poland, Finland and the Baltic States, the inhabitants of the old Russian Empire found themselves in so-called Union or Autonomous Republics. Although these Republics exercised theoretical powers, effectively Russia dominated the Federation, which is precisely what Stalin intended. Lenin became concerned, particularly at the way in which Stalin rode roughshod over national aspirations in his native Georgia. Lenin complained about 'Great Russian Chauvinism', but he was too ill to fight his cause effectively. Lenin's influence was evident in the 1923 Constitution, which deliberately referred to a 'Union of Soviet

Socialist Republics', without specifically mentioning Russia. But Lenin had not fought hard enough, and he had taken up the cause too late. It was Stalin's perception of the Constitution which prevailed. Although it was a few years before Stalin embarked upon a policy of Russification, attempting to eliminate separate national characteristics, the framework was already in place before Lenin's death.

LENIN AS THEORIST AND PHILOSOPHER

Lenin firmly believed that policy should rest upon correct philosophical foundations, and therefore he devoted a considerable portion of his writings to an investigation of those foundations. The importance he attached to this work helps to explain the vigour with which Lenin attacked fellow Socialists like the German Kautsky, Socialists who he believed were guilty of bad Marxism. Lenin's convictions bordered upon arrogance. He certainly conveyed the impression on several occasions that only he was capable of fully understanding and interpreting Marx. Yet Lenin himself was capable of contradictions, and he also changed his stance on several issues, so he did not leave an entirely coherent political philosophy any more than Marx himself did. It is hardly surprising, since as an active politician, Lenin tended to act and then produce theoretical justifications afterwards – scarcely a new phenomenon in politics. This is not to say that Lenin did not genuinely believe in his public pronouncements at any particular time.

Whatever criticisms might be made of Lenin as a thinker, his influence as an interpreter of Marxism was unquestionably great. This is partly due to Lenin's philosophy itself, and partly because his thoughts were accepted as gospel truth by later generations of Communists both inside and outside the Soviet Union. Marx was recognised by Soviet scholars as the founder of 'scientific Communism', since he attempted a 'scientific' analysis of past societies and the nineteenth-century capitalism of his own lifetime, rather than following in the footsteps of the 'utopian Socialists' of his era. Marx combined a study of philosophy, political economy and 'scientific Communism' to formulate economic 'laws' such as the two-stage transition from capitalism to Communism. Lenin saw his task as developing and refining Marx's ideas in order to make them a relevant tool for analysing conditions in Russia, and in the changing world generally.

Many of Lenin's early writings were polemical, directed at developments in Socialist thinking which he claimed were a deviation from Marxism. But in addition to interpreting Marx, he also wrote about areas which had been less central to his predecessor. Thus, for example, Lenin devoted some of his work to formulating laws of capitalist development in agriculture, important in a country in which the great majority of people still derived their living directly from the land. He also wrote about those economic and political developments which seemed more important to the generation of Marxists who came after Marx – for example the concentration and monopolisation of capital, and imperialism, which appeared to be transferring the inner contradictions of capitalism to the international stage. Lenin also wrote more than Marx about the transition period from capitalism to Socialism, because it was directly relevant to the situation in which he and his colleagues found themselves in 1917 and later years.

However, Lenin's most important legacy as a theorist was probably his analysis of the role of Communist Parties in acting as the vanguard of the proletariat, bringing about revolution, and managing the transition to Socialism. Lenin's ideas on the role of the Party, and his views on the means by which economically-backward countries could move towards Socialism without going through the full and drawn-out capitalist stage of development, were an inspiration to later generations of revolutionaries. This is true whether they fully understood his ideas or not. All religions, Marxism-Leninism included, rely as much upon faith as rational explanation, and a simplistic interpretation of Lenin's ideas and an awareness of his career had an appeal for individuals and groups seeking successful revolutionary change in their own societies. This remained so even after Stalin put his own gloss on the ideas of Marx and Lenin and forbade any deviation from the official Party line. Whatever criticisms might be made of the 'scientific' nature of some of Lenin's ideas, the fact that they were prescribed for generations of Soviet citizens, and were taken up by enthusiastic comrades abroad, marks Lenin out not just as a remarkable political leader but a modern prophet who could not be ignored by friend or foe alike.

Points to consider

1) Was Lenin more important as a theorist or a man of action?
2) How did Lenin deal with the issue of State power and the bureaucracy?
3) What were Lenin's views on the non-Russian nationalities and how successfully did he handle national relationships within the Soviet Union?
4) What adaptations did Lenin make to Marxism?
5) How successful had Lenin been as the Soviet Union's leader by the time of his death in 1924?
6) Why was Lenin so influential after his death?

7

HISTORIOGRAPHY

EARLY SOVIET HISTORIOGRAPHY
—

Lenin became a subject for serious political commentators only after the October Revolution in 1917. Until then he excited interest only amongst relatively few Russians, including the tsarist secret police, and a few foreign Socialists. His name was occasionally mentioned in foreign newspapers after his return to Russia in April 1917, but the information given was very vague. Little was known about him. His reputation amongst foreign and Russian Socialists was that of an argumentative individual, forever threatening to create splits in the revolutionary movement. It is not surprising that little was known about Lenin the person. Although Lenin was a prolific writer, he wrote little about his own background, even the reasons why he had become a revolutionary in the first place. His books had not been read outside Socialist circles, and it was difficult to ascertain what he really stood for. Although Lenin was discussed at some length in Russia in the summer of 1917, it was mostly in connection with his involvement with the German authorities, who has assisted in his transporation back to Russia.

In 1918, in Petrograd, Lenin's colleague, Zinoviev, published the first known biography of Russia's new leader. It was scarcely known outside Russia. Yet there was now a marked transformation of public interest in Lenin. He had achieved worldwide notoriety almost overnight, and references to him in print, on posters, and in film, multiplied. The Soviet practice of renaming streets and buildings after political leaders was begun, although Petrograd itself was not to become Leningrad until after Lenin's death. However, this interest in Lenin created a problem which has only recently begun to be addressed in post-Soviet Russia: Lenin was as much a symbol as a person, and this fact was to colour so many interpretations of him both within and beyond his own country. From the beginning, opinions about Lenin were bound up with opinions about the Russian Revolution. To Communists Lenin was above criticism, at least publically, especially once it was certain that his hold on power in Russia was more than a passing phase. Anti-Communists transferred their fear and loathing of Communism on to the man, so it was convenient to make him a devil figure. 'German spy', 'Jewish conspirator', 'plague bacillus' were amongst the more polite epithets. Even serious historians found it difficult to separate the man and the symbol.

The first edition of Lenin's *Collected Works*, which were considerable, was compiled in 1920. The writings revealed only a partial view of the man. The deification of Lenin began well before his death, much to his own embarrassment. Objectivity was rendered even more impossible by the haste with which Lenin's colleagues, after his death, seized every opportunity to legitimise their own ideas and actions by invoking the authority of his name. Stalin was to become a master of this art.

Serious studies of Lenin, including biographical details, began to appear. Trotsky's *Lenin* was published in 1925. Although Trotsky was very conscious of his own significant role in 1917, he generously conceded in later books that Lenin's personal contribution to the success of the Revolution had been crucial. Although it went somewhat against the Marxist grain, Trotsky ventured the opinion that without Lenin the Bolshevik Party might not have seized its opportunity:

> The conditions of war and revolution . . . would not allow the Party a long period for fulfilling its mission. Thus it is by no means excluded that a disoriented and split Party might have let slip the revolutionary opportunity for many years. The role of the personality arises before us here on a truly gigantic scale.
>
> (L. Trotsky, *History of the Russian Revolution*)

Krupskaya wrote a biography of Lenin in 1927. It should have provided useful insights, but she was reticent on several matters, and in any case her manuscript was revised by the Party. Soviet censors were very adept at rewriting history.

LATER SOVIET INTERPRETATIONS

Soviet references to Lenin in the 1930s were on the level of uncritical hagiography, designed mostly to bathe Stalin in reflected glory. Serious study of Lenin within the USSR began properly in 1953, the year of Stalin's death. The denunciation of Stalin and his abuses of power in 1956 awakened an interest in Lenin other than as a symbol. Stalin's denunciators, such as Khrushchev, were at pains to demonstrate that Stalin had perverted Lenin's ideas, and that the reforms being proposed in the 1950s and early 1960s were firmly in line with Leninist principles. Research was stimulated, and new editions of Lenin's *Collected Works* were begun. The library shelves groaned under the weight as previously unpublished articles were discovered. Even to this day not all of Lenin's writings have been published: some are still locked in Russian archives.

An official Party biography of Lenin was published in 1963. *Vladimir Ilyich Lenin*, by P.N. Pospelov, presented Lenin as the one infallible successor to Marx, and an original and saintly master not just of politics but virtually every other facet of human life. Objective history it definitely was not.

Renewed Soviet interest in Lenin continued throughout the 1970s and beyond. The Central V. I. Lenin Museum in Moscow has always taken great pride in displaying the 55 volumes of Lenin's *Collected Works* (Fifth Edition), published between 1958 and 1964. *The CPSU (Communist Party of the Soviet Union), The Ideological, Political and Organisational Principles*, published in Moscow in 1982, was a detailed commentary on the role of the Party as the leading force in Soviet life in the 65 years since the Revolution. Throughout its pages the name of Lenin was constantly invoked to lend authority to the activities of the Party. Stalin, of course, was not mentioned, it being the post-Stalinist era. The following brief extract is typical of the tone:

> One can rightfully say that today, too, Lenin is a living participant in all CPSU affairs, is its reliable and wise ideological teacher and sagacious preceptor.

In 1978 the then General Secretary of the Communist Party, Brezhnev, published *Pressing Problems of the CPSU Ideological Work*. The book was replete with ringing tributes to Lenin, Brezhnev doubtless hoping that some of Lenin's aura would rub off on himself. Brezhnev praised Lenin's contribution to the development of the Party, his 'penetrating and profound' theoretical thinking. Lenin had been 'a man totally free of the slightest semblance of dogmatism.' He was 'a consistent opponent of any adventurism, a flexible and circumspect politician . . . a model of revolutionary boldness, resoluteness, and purposefulness'. And yet at the same time Lenin had been 'a man of spotless purity, and of exceptional personal charm'. How could one man have had so many qualities and have achieved so much? Brezhnev forestalled the sceptics by insisting upon Lenin's 'staggering capacity for work' and his 'tireless, persevering efficiency and indomitable will; the erudition and keen mind of the great scientist with a sincere love of life, of its true values and joys.'

Three years later the Soviet historian Y. Kukushkin continued the eulogies, concluding in his *History of the USSR* that every achievement of the Soviet people on the road to Socialism 'contains a particle of Lenin's genius, his titanic, almost super-human work'.

There was much purple prose, but little good history in these outpourings. A change in Soviet perceptions of Lenin, particularly concerning his role after 1917, did become evident in the mid 1980s, the years of *Glasnost* and *Perestroika*. For the first time there was, for example, criticism of some of the excesses of the Civil War period, including the butchery of the tsar and his family. Although criticism of Lenin was implied rather than overt, there was the beginning of a debate about the extent to which some of the features of the Stalinist period, with all its arbitrariness and harshness, had already been present in the period between 1918 and 1921. However, historians tended to be more critical of other individuals like Dzerzhinsky, Head of the CHEKA, and Trotsky. There was still a tendency to use Lenin as a yardstick against which to measure and analyse other politicians. There was a noticeable attempt, encouraged by Gorbachev himself, to present Lenin's introduction of NEP in 1921 as on a par with the market reforms which were part of mid-1980s *Perestroika*. Gorbachev was very critical of the ruthlessness of the Stalin years and the stagnation of the Brezhnev era, but insisted that his own policies were a return to the virtues of democratic Leninism. Although Lenin had insisted upon a disciplined Party organisation, it was emphasised that in the true spirit of democratic Socialism, he had been prepared to discuss ideas with critics in Party circles in a way that

Stalin never allowed. Nevertheless, although Lenin was used as a commentary upon the present, there was at least the beginnings of a demythologising of the man. In 1987 a Soviet historian, Polyakov, in reply to the question 'Will Lenin ever be portrayed as a multidimensional figure who also made definite mistakes?', stated, 'For the time being we are ashamed to speak about this, and, I think, wrongly so.' But criticisms did emerge. One was a questioning of Lenin's ban on factions in 1921, despite the fact that for decades the role of the unitary and united Party had always been accepted as gospel:

> The overwhelming majority accepted into the Party from non-proletarian classes were of course honest, and devoted to the people. But the trouble was that because of their insufficient class and political maturity they were a favourable medium for the advance of all kinds of adventurist, careerist and similar elements. Unfortunately this was assisted by the resolution of the Tenth Congress 'On The Unity Of The Party'. It firmly blocked any real and serious opposition to the line of the leader of the Party because it provided for 'the complete elimination of any factional activity', for which the punishment was pitiless. But internal Party practice then showed that any criticism of the leadership could be arbitrarily included in 'factional activity', if the criticism came from several Party members.
>
> (A. Burganov, *Druzhba Narodov* 1988)

The implication was clear: Lenin had prepared the ground for Stalin or someone like him to advance to power after his own demise.

A vigorous debate about Lenin did open up, and professional historians were prominent in the arguments. Many still took the line that Lenin's faults and mistakes arose largely from force of circumstance rather than incompetence or malevolence. Russian historians now have a more realistic understanding of Lenin, recognising for example that his influence was greater at some times than at others. Many of the documentary sources relating to Lenin's career have yet to be released, so it is still difficult for Russian historians, now freed from ideological constraints, to compile a fully-rounded picture of the man. However, it can at least be said that the days of unqualified hagiography of Lenin are over.

EARLY WESTERN HISTORIOGRAPHY

Foreign, particularly Western, studies of Lenin also found it difficult to separate the man from the symbol. There was a much wider range of opinions about Lenin, ranging from the adulation of foreign Communists to the hatred or fear expressed by virulent anti-Marxists.

Early foreign press reports about Lenin were simply propaganda. Journalists had few facts to go on even if they cared about establishing the truth. Lenin was variously portrayed as a German spy, a madman, a Jewish activist, an Antichrist. Foreign visitors met Lenin in Moscow for the first time in 1918. The British Labour politician George Lansbury commented upon his humanity – 'The gentle Lenin' – whilst H.G. Wells in 1920 found him unprepossessing both in appearance and in his writings. George Bernard Shaw praised his intellectual powers. Winston Churchill, a strong opponent of Communism, wrote of Lenin as a destroyer of human society, although he conceded that Lenin's death in 1924 was probably a disaster for Russia, in view of what was to come later.

Throughout the 1920s and early 1930s Western commentators were heavily influenced in their opinions of Lenin by their own political persuasion. The French writer Henri Barbusse wrote that Lenin 'is one of the most all-embracing and integral personalities that ever existed.' He went on:

> He guided modern thought, that wandered in the blind alleys of futile seekings onto the path of creative endeavour and practical application, impregnating it with revolutionary logic and revolutionary truth.

Katayama, organiser of the Japanese Communist Party, listened to Lenin's speech at the Ninth All-Russian Congress of the Soviets in 1921:

> Comrade Lenin did not resort to bombast or any gestures, but he possessed an immense personal magnetism; when he began to speak complete silence fell over the hall; all eyes were upon him. Comrade Lenin would glance at the audience as if hypnotising it. I watched the big crowd and did not see a single person move or hear a cough during those three hours . . . Comrade Lenin is the greatest speaker I have ever heard.

Martin Anderson, a Danish participant at the Fourth Comintern Congress held in 1921, was overwhelmed by Lenin:

> Lenin's appearance, his simple manner revealed him as a man of a new epoch. Talking to him, everybody, the simplest of folk, felt he was confronting one of those extraordinary people who are only born once in a hundred or perhaps even once in a thousand years.

Bertrand Russell, writing on the occasion of Lenin's death in 1924, was equally impressed:

> Lenin's death deprives the world of the only truly great man engendered by the War ... He had a harmonious creative mind. He was a philosopher, a creator of a system in the field of practice ... He combined in himself a sharp orthodoxy of thought and the ability to adjust to reality; he never made any concessions which would have an aim other than the ultimate triumph of Communism.

Many of the commentaries were written by convinced admirers or opponents, and there were few serious attempts to actually analyse Lenin's ideology or practical achievements.

After Lenin's death there were for many years only a few full-length studies of the man and his influence, as opposed to brief recollections such as those quoted above. Few historians could claim to have known Lenin personally, and a limited amount of documentary material was available. One of the first serious studies of Lenin written outside the Soviet Union was George Vernadsky's *Lenin, Red Dictator*, published in 1931. Although written in the United States, the author was a Russian emigré. Vernadsky had his own axe to grind against the Russian Revolution, and he regarded Lenin as a tyrant responsible for innumerable deaths. However, as an historian aiming to be objective he was not prepared to pass final judgement on the Lenin years without the benefit of greater perspective.

LATER WESTERN HISTORIOGRAPHY

During the 1930s and the Second World War, foreign interest in Soviet personalities centred more upon Stalin than Lenin. But the international importance of the USSR in the era of the Cold War re-awakened a scholarly interest in Stalin's predecessor. A number of distinguished writers tackled Lenin's life and influence, although few of them were professional historians.

David Schub's *Lenin* appeared in 1948. Schub had joined the Social Democratic Party in 1903, then emigrated to America in 1908. His book drew upon personal contacts with the revolutionary movement and a range of primary sources. Schub's study is detailed but at times relies upon gossip as much as authentic contemporary sources.

Bertram Wolfe was an American Communist who had lived in Moscow for two years during the 1920s. He published *Three Who Made a Revolution* in 1948. The three were Lenin, Trotsky and Stalin. Unfortunately, although Wolfe had known Trotsky and Stalin personally, he had never met Lenin. Nevertheless, his was one of the first serious analyses of Lenin.

Louis Fischer published his *Life of Lenin* in 1964. Fischer was a well-known newspaper correspondent who had lived in the USSR during the 1920s and 1930s. Fischer was not a Communist. He wrote chiefly about foreign affairs and did not produce major insights into Lenin.

Adam Ulam published *The Bolsheviks* in 1965. Polish by birth, Ulam came to hold an academic post in the United States and wrote in detail about Lenin's ideas and policies, although the history of the Bolshevik Party rather than Lenin himself was his principal interest.

Christopher Hill

The English Marxist historian Christopher Hill wrote *Lenin and the Russian Revolution* in 1947. Hill was very sympathetic to Lenin both as a man and as a politician, and passed very favourable judgements on what he achieved for Russia. At the time, popular feeling in Britain towards the recent wartime ally was still warm. Hill was interested in Lenin both as a man and a symbol. Lenin 'first and foremost . . . symbolises the Russian Revolution as a movement of the poor and oppressed of the earth who have successfully risen against the great and the powerful.'

Lenin the man, despite his upbringing, 'was very close to the common average Russian'. Lenin was fundamentally democratic and humane, a man who was afraid to listen to beautiful music too often because it made him 'want to say stupid, nice things, and stroke the heads of people who would create such beauty while living in this vile hell'. Hill also saw Lenin as a Russian patriot, for all his statements in favour of internationalism, someone who freed Russia from foreign domination.

It is doubtful whether Lenin would have recognised these interpretations of himself, but Hill's portrait was very much of its time, and was influenced by his conviction that the Russian Revolution itself 'uplifted the poor and the downtrodden and improved their lot in the everyday things of life'. Hill is a respected historian of seventeenth-century England, but his perceptions of Lenin were simplistic and frequently misleading. They are worth noting as an example of how sympathetic Western commentators could swallow the official Soviet line, albeit a watered-down version.

E. H. Carr

E. H. Carr's massive *History of Soviet Russia*, published between 1950 and 1964, was an analysis of the institutions which emerged in the Soviet Union after the Revolution. Carr was not particularly concerned with individuals, but he did pay tribute to Lenin as a great revolutionary, whose main contribution was not to overthrow the tsar or the Provisional Government in 1917, but rather to try to come to terms with the difficult situation in which Russia found itself after 1917. Carr was certainly impressed by the institutions which Lenin founded, but offered no personal insights into Lenin, and wrote in as detached a way as possible. His detachment led him to accept a lot at face value. Carr was not very sympathetic to Lenin the ruler, since he admired bureaucratic efficiency and many administrative features which became associated with Stalinism, and he did not agree with all Lenin's reservations on the subject. Carr's interest in historical trends rather than individuals ironically came closer to the Marxist ideal of History analysed in terms of impersonal forces rather than individuals, whereas Soviet historians seemed far more concerned to focus on Lenin's personal contribution to the Bolshevik victory and its aftermath.

Leonard Schapiro

Leonard Schapiro was representative of the view which was very critical of Lenin in several respects, and saw his system very much as the forerunner of Stalinism. Schapiro claimed to be avoiding value judgements, but he made them anyway: 'Lenin and his followers were less interested in doctrine that in preserving their own rule' was one such judgement. Lenin's obsession with power 'proved the only durable element in his thought'. Schapiro contradicted himself by interpreting Lenin as an idealist: 'He had a natural asceticism of character which power did not corrupt, and he could do evil without losing sight of the ultimate good in which he believed'. But he naively expected his followers to do likewise. Lenin wanted harmony, but he suffered from a 'rigid inability to see facts except within the framework of his own dogma . . . He knew of only one role in politics: no compromise with opponents and no adoption of their policy or views until you have first destroyed them'. (L. Schapiro, *The Communist Party Of The Soviet Union* 1964.) Therefore, concluded Schapiro, Lenin was a great revolutionary figure but he could not be called a statesman.

Robert Daniels

The American historian Robert Daniels was convinced that Lenin's lust for power was the key to understanding the Revolution itself. Lenin was victorious in October 1917 as the fortuitous result of a series of chances, but his method of achieving power precluded a democratic result. October was a 'wild gamble'. However, Daniels conceded that Lenin's leadership probably was decisive in the hour of crisis. It was irrelevant to speculate whether Lenin's regime could have been established with a less violent outcome:

> Given the fact of the party's forcible seizure of power, civil violence and a militarised dictatorship of revolutionary extremism followed with a remorseless logic.
>
> (R. Daniels, *Red October. The Bolshevik Revolution* 1967)

Marcel Liebmann

Many of the writers analysed above believed that events in Russia could not have proceeded in the way that they did without Lenin. Many writers agreed on his qualities. Where disagreement emerged, it was often about the sense or rightness of Lenin's policies, and whether the cost in terms of lives and damage to Russia was not too great to justify. As serious analyses of Stalinism were written, historians considered the extent to which Lenin was responsible for that which came after him.

The French historian Marcel Liebmann made a detailed study of Lenin's thought and career. *Leninism Under Lenin* was published in 1975. As a sympathiser, Liebmann was anxious to exonerate Lenin from the charge that he had implemented a totalitarian regime inherited by Stalin. Changes in policy by Lenin were treated not as demonstrating a lack of principle, but 'a high level of tactical sensitivity and a refusal to let himself be imprisoned in principles.' Although Lenin showed authoritarian tendencies:

> Let there be no misconception, however: the authority that Lenin enjoyed had nothing dictatorial about it, and if he sometimes sought to impose on his followers an attitude of unconditional acceptance, he aimed in doing this not so much at ensuring allegiance to himself personally as at obtaining unity around a theory that he believed to be correct.

This interpretation smacks of special pleading: most dictators can find good reasons for implementing authoritarian policies. However, Liebmann's assessment of Lenin was more balanced in other respects. He accepted that Lenin had failed to resolve several problems, such as how to implement Socialist democracy. He recognised that 'the bureaucratic and totalitarian degeneration of the Soviet regime' began before Lenin's death. But Liebmann was concerned to show the differences between Leninism and Stalinism, even their basic incompatibility. For example, Lenin tried, if unsuccessfully, to restrict the power of the bureaucracy. Liebmann claimed that Lenin's own authority was not buttressed by Terror, as was Stalin's. This was a rather dubious interpretation. Liebmann was also led into the dangerous game of predicting what Lenin *would* have done had he lived longer. He thought, for example, that Lenin would have taken the Bukharinite conciliatory line towards the peasants during the economic debates of the mid and late 1920s. He would have been not only less brutal than Stalin, but also more sensitive in his perception of the sensitivities of the international situation. This argument is not convincing. It is true that Lenin sometimes talked in terms of influencing the peasants 'morally', rather than using force, but during his lifetime Lenin made dramatic changes of course when he felt that the situation demanded it – just as Stalin was to. Liebmann was correct in criticising attempts to portray Stalinism as a straight continuation of Leninism. Such an interpretation would be simplistic. Stalin steered Russia on a particular course, assisted by a new generation of ambitious Communists. The Old Guard was virtually wiped out in the Purges. Although Lenin, as we have seen, could be ruthless, he did not turn Soviet Communism into a religion of national development in the way Stalin did; and he did not rewrite history and deliberately stimulate a climate of suspicion and insecurity as Stalin was to do in the 1930s. Lenin had enough real problems to deal with. He did not create many of the problems, although some of them he made worse, and some occurred because of the path by which Lenin seized power. Lenin did achieve remarkable feats, and perhaps attempts to denigrate the achievements are in part a natural reaction to the uncritical adulation which he received in Soviet propaganda in the decades after his death.

LATER ASSESSMENTS

More recent assessments of Lenin have been reasonably balanced, as perspective lengthens, and more evidence emerges from the archives. Lenin can now be viewed as a rounded individual, someone who made a great impact on Russian and world history, but who was a man of faults as well as virtues, whose contribution should be considered without the need to indulge in polemic or propaganda.

Geoffrey Hosking in 1990 could assess Lenin in the context of a disintegrating Soviet Union and with a long-term perspective:

> To a greater extent than is usually realised, Lenin was a divided personality. He shared with previous Russian revolutionaries the belief in a humane and democratic future society. Where he differed from them was in hard-headed realism and

the determination to achieve power at all costs. He craved a historical theory which would provide absolute certainty, and in Marxism he thought he had found it. 'Marxism is all-powerful because it is *true*', as he was fond of repeating. The unacknowledged and ultimately incongruous mixture of science and prophecy in Marxism was exactly what appealed to Lenin, and to solve the mismatch between them he invented the 'party' as a hierarchical and disciplined organisation dedicated to exercising power in the name of a proletariat which could never do so.

(G. Hosking, *A History of the Soviet Union* 1990)

In the same year Edward Acton gave a similarly balanced interpretation. He rightly drew attention to the importance of Lenin's role in developing a Party organisation, whilst emphasising that

'he was in no position to impose policy upon the party'. The fact that Lenin's policies were adopted owed as much to the fact that they were in accordance with rank-and-file radicalism as to Lenin's own persuasiveness. 'The stamp he set upon party policy reflected the close correspondence between his programme and the demands welling up from below. Acton was convinced that Lenin did have a genuine belief in popular radicalism, reinforced by the experience of 1917. He claims that too much attention has been devoted to Lenin's relationship with the Party, when 'the party was neither at the beck and call of Lenin nor was it an élite group of intellectuals divorced from the masses ... "Bolshevism" in 1917 did not flow from a single fount but embraced many different currents of thought.' Likewise, this multi-faceted Party had a variety of answers to the many problems that emerged after 1917, problems mostly underestimated by Lenin. Lenin therefore was not an all-powerful dictator, and if he is criticised, perhaps it should be on the grounds of 'ill-founded optimism' rather than 'insincerity.'

(*E. Acton, Rethinking the Russian Revolution* 1990)

A similarly balanced and rounded view of Lenin is evident in Robert Service's three volume *Lenin: A Political Life*, published in the 1980s and 1990s. Service shows at length the difficult relationship which Lenin had with colleagues in the Party, and how Lenin's impact on events has sometimes been exaggerated. 'If Lenin had never existed, a socialist government would probably still have ruled Russia by the end of the year.' (R. Service, *Lenin: A Political Life Volume 2* 1991). Service emphasises that one reason for Lenin's pre-eminence among the Bolsheviks was his ability to assess when ideological considerations were most important, and when practical ones were. It is a far more convincing portrait of the man, warts and all, than many earlier polemical studies.

Both the passage of time and the transformation of the old Soviet Union have given us a new perspective on Soviet history and Lenin's part in it. It is easier for us to be dispassionate, although of course there is no guarantee that we can achieve total objectivity – we are as much a product of the prejudices of our own times as Lenin's contemporaries and earlier historians were of theirs. There will continue to be disagreements about Lenin, even if we do achieve a more rounded picture, based as far as possible on analysis without personal prejudice. A wise old historian, A.J.P. Taylor, remarked: 'Everyone can have his private tastes, but they can have no place in historical study.' Historical study without prejudice should still be interesting. Let us leave the last words with Lenin, in *Left Wing Communism*:

> History generally, and the history of revolutions in particular, is always richer in content, more varied, more many-sided, more lively and more 'subtle' than even the best parties and the most class-conscious vanguards of the most advanced classes imagine.

Points to consider

1) **What difficulties are there for a historian in writing the life of Lenin?**
2) **Assess the strengths and limitations of any historical study of Lenin with which you are familiar.**

BIBLIOGRAPHY

There are many relevant books on the history of Russia and the Soviet Union during Lenin's lifetime, but the following are just a few books particularly useful for a study of Lenin himself.

R. Appignanesi and O. Zarate, *Lenin For Beginners* (Writers and Readers Publishing Cooperative, 1977)

H. Carrère d'Encausse, *Lenin: Revolution and Power* (Longman, 1982)

T. Cliff, *Lenin* 4 volumes (Pluto Press, 1975–9)

I. Deutscher, *Lenin's Childhood* (Oxford University Press, 1970)

V. Lenin, *What is to be Done?* (Penguin, 1988)

M. Liebmann, *Leninism Under Lenin* (Merlin Press, 1980)

S. Possony, *Lenin, the Compulsive Revolutionary* (Allen and Unwin, 1966)

T. Rigby, *Lenin's Government: Sovnarkom 1917–22* (Cambridge University Press, 1979)

R. Service, *Lenin, a Political Life*, 2 Volumes thus far (Macmillan, 1985, 1991)

R. C. Tucker, *The Lenin Anthology* (New York, Norton 1975)

INDEX